REMOVALS

REMOVALS

*Nineteenth-Century
American Literature and
the Politics of Indian Affairs*

LUCY MADDOX

New York   Oxford
OXFORD UNIVERSITY PRESS
1991

Oxford University Press

Oxford   New York   Toronto
Delhi   Bombay   Calcutta   Madras   Karachi
Petaling Jaya   Singapore   Hong Kong   Tokyo
Nairobi   Dar es Salaam   Cape Town
Melbourne   Auckland

and associated companies in
Berlin   Ibadan

Copyright © 1991 by Oxford University Press, Inc.

Published by Oxford University Press, Inc.,
200 Madison Avenue, New York, New York 10016

Oxford is a registered trademark of Oxford University Press

Library of Congress Cataloging-in-Publication Data
Maddox, Lucy.
Removals : nineteenth-century American literature and the politics
of Indian affairs / Lucy Maddox.
p.   cm.   Includes bibliographical references and index.
ISBN 0-19-506931-5
1. American literature—19th century—History and criticism.
2. Indians of North America—Politics and government—History—19th century.
3. Politics and literature—United States—History—19th century.
4. Indians in literature. 5. Canon (Literature) I. Title.
PS173.I6M3   1991
810.9'358'09034—dc20   90-21547

2 4 6 8 9 7 5 3 1

Printed in the United States of America
on acid-free paper

Acknowledgments

THE WRITING of a book is always, to some extent, a collaborative effort. I want to acknowledge briefly some of those whom I consider to have been my most important collaborators, whether they meant to be or not.

My colleague George O'Brien generously read a full draft of the manuscript and filled the margins with sharp-eyed comments and questions; his incisive marginalia became my primary guide to revision. Other colleagues—especially Susan Lanser, Michael Ragussis, Penn Szittya, John Glavin, John Hirsh, and Lynn Thiesmeyer—supplied encouragement, interest, informed conversation, and good questions. My students, both at Georgetown University and at the Bread Loaf School of English, kept me on my intellectual toes; they also kept me constantly aware of the importance as well as the excitement of learning to read old texts in new ways. The administration of Georgetown University granted me a year's sabbatical leave that allowed me to do most of the research for the book. Lynne Hirschfeld and Joan Reuss cheerfully and skillfully guided me through the frustrations of disk errors, document merges, formats, and paper jams. Jim Maddox patiently answered all my questions: how to spell a word, whether a phrase made sense, how long Martin

Van Buren was in office. Maggy Lindgren, Sam Swope, Nancy Martin, and Dixie Goswami kept asking me how it was going and then listening, with apparent interest, as I explained at length how it was going.

Everyone should have such collaborators.

Washington, D.C.   L. M.
April 1991

Contents

REMOVALS

Introduction

THE FULL STORY of Indian-white relations in North America is beginning to be told. But the emerging story is already taking two different forms. One version is being produced through the collaboration of a variety of traditionally white academic disciplines: history, anthropology, ethnography, sociology, even literary criticism. The same matter is simultaneously being treated from an Indian perspective, through academic programs in Native American Studies and, especially, through the recent proliferation of works by Indian writers that mark what has already been called the Native American Renaissance. Thus far, however, the two versions of the story remain separated by fundamental differences in the very nature of their structure and their discourse; it is still difficult to imagine a merging of the two into a single text. The definition of American history that the academy has always found most usable has been able, so far, to accommodate only an admittedly ethnocentric version of Indian history. Similarly, our working definition of American literature has not yet been able to accommodate Indian texts, oral or written, very comfortably. And these prevailing definitions, of course, not only determine their own discourses but continue to privilege them over competing ones.

The problem of bringing the two discourses together remains a

troubling one. Those of us who are in the relevant academic disciplines have still not made up our collective mind about whether it is
appropriate to aim for a converging of the two versions of the story,
or even whether such a convergence is possible. We have not, in fact,
even decided whether the privileging of one discourse over another
is a form of cultural arrogance that limits our knowledge, or whether
it is the most logical and efficient way of extending the knowledge
we already have.

The polarizing of positions that questions of this kind can produce
is well illustrated by the first two essays in a collection called *The
American Indian and the Problem of History*, a book that sets out
to address the specific question of whether a single version of American history is possible or whether there must always be at least two
American histories. In the first essay, a historian argues that it is not
only possible but necessary for academic historians to unlearn their
ethnocentric methodologies and learn to merge Indian and white
"metaphysics" into a single, "bicultural" understanding of the past:
"The time is auspicious to equip ourselves with the linguist's and
ethnologist's tools and to return to the sources and find the Indian
as he defined himself and his world."[1] In the second essay, another
historian argues that even if such a "bicultural" approach were possible, it would not produce valid history-writing:

> Only the end of writing formal history as we know it can truly ac-
> complish the cross-cultural goals implied by the metaphysics of writing
> Indian history. Can we, however, throw out the ethnocentric bath-
> water of Indian history without also tossing out the baby of history?
> . . . History-as-understanding and history-writing are parts of specific
> cultures, hence ethnocentric in their presuppositions about the nature
> and ordering of the past-as-lived. Without these constraints, there can
> be no formal history-as-now-understood; with those constraints there
> can be no New Indian History as some envision its larger goals of
> cross-cultural respect and understanding.[2]

In short, according to this latter argument, American history (as text)
cannot accommodate Indian history (as text) without destroying itself. The two discourses must remain separate; and if they do, the
passage implies, then it follows that, at least among academic his-

torians, the relative values of the (white) baby and the (Indian) bathwater will remain constant.

Among teachers and critics of literature, there are similar differences of opinion about whether Indian texts, either oral or written, can be made accessible to a non-Indian audience through any of the methodological approaches currently available in academic literary studies—or, for that matter, whether many of the Indian materials can even be legitimately treated as *texts*. Arnold Krupat represents one side of this argument when he says that although "to speak of post-structuralist theory in conjunction with Native American literatures may seem as odd as serving dog stew with *sauce bearnaise*" the emphasis in poststructuralist theory on interpretive openness and indeterminate meanings actually makes it a useful and appropriate methodological tool for illuminating Indian literatures, especially oral narratives.[3] On the other side of the argument are those who, like Elaine Jahner, caution that "critics need to be aware that conventional approaches and vocabulary are as likely to obscure as to illuminate" both the form and the content of Native literature, oral or written.[4] The most radical argument against the position represented by Krupat can be illustrated, very succinctly, by Gerald Vizenor's insistence that "academic evidence is a euphemism for linguistic colonization of oral traditions and popular memories."[5]

This contemporary argument among academics about the compatibility of competing discourses actually has a long and fairly stable genealogy; what distinguishes this newest version of the argument from previous versions is primarily its narrowness, its location almost entirely within the academic community. Although the argument now focuses on the admission of Native American history and literature(s) into the canon and the curriculum, what was at issue in earlier phases of the debate was the admission of the Indian people themselves into the structures of American society. Then as now, the voices that have dominated the discussion have begun with the assumption that accommodation really means the complete assimilation of the Indians into white institutions. And over and over, those voices have declared that they find such accommodation ultimately impossible. As President James Monroe put it in 1825, "Experience has clearly demonstrated that, in their present state, it is impossible to incorporate [the Indians] in such masses, in any form whatever, into our systems."[6] Monroe's conclusion was echoed by John Quincy Adams in 1828; in the history of official relations with the Indians to that date, Adams said, "the ultimate design was to incorporate in our own institutions that portion of them which could be converted to the state of civilization."[7] Having given up on the design of incorporation, both Monroe and Adams eventually settled on a new design: the removal of the Indians beyond the limits of the "systems" and "institutions" of white civilization.

In the current debates over the status of Indian literature and history in our academic institutions, we have not, I believe, fully acknowledged just how long the basic terms of the argument have been in place. Nor have we fully recognized something even more important: the "Indian question" that now seems mildly perplexing to some of us was much more deeply perplexing to those who were concerned with the definitions of American literature and history in the first half of the nineteenth century, when those definitions were still being constructed and when the fate of the Indians was still being decided. The question of whether Indians and whites could inhabit the same territory, physical or metaphysical, was unavoidable as long as the Indians continued to defend their right to live (and to maintain their tribal identities) within the territorial limits of the United States; it was a question that had to be confronted by anyone who participated—whether by moving to the frontier, by becoming a candidate for office or even voting for one, or by publishing a book—in the extension of the claims of white culture to full possession of the country. Yet, in our reading of nineteenth-century literature, we have generally assumed that only a handful of writers were actively concerned with the politics or the ideology of Indian-white relationships, and that the only major one among them was James Fenimore Cooper; the rest were minor frontier writers, western local colorists, or negligible sentimentalists. Such an assumption is, I believe, the equivalent of concluding that the only American works of the 1960s and 1970s to which the Vietnam War is relevant are those that are set in Vietnam.

My study of "the Indian question" focuses primarily (although not exclusively) on the period between 1830, when the U.S. Congress officially sanctioned the creation of an Indian Territory west of the Mississippi and the removal of the Indians still living east of the Mississippi, and the middle of the 1850s, when the attention of the general public shifted from the problem of the Indians to the problems of slavery and sectionalism. The establishment of the Indian Territory in 1830 was clearly an attempt to obviate the problem of Indian-white incompatibility by simply drawing dividing lines across the map of North America. But it was just as clearly a shortsighted attempt (or perhaps a deliberately temporizing expedient), since white Americans soon began to push beyond the geographical boundaries they had set for themselves, insisting that wherever they went, they brought with them the rights and privileges to which they were entitled by virtue of their status as citizens of the United States. Whereas the presence of Indians in the East had originally been an obstacle to the construction of a morally defensible American polity and to the enforcement of federal and state laws, their presence in the West quickly proved to be an obstacle to white America's claims to the moral right to unhindered expansion across the continent. The Indians, that is, continued to frustrate white America's efforts—official and unofficial—to include them within the discourse of American nationalism and, concomitantly, within the structure of the country's laws and institutions.

In his report for the year 1851, the Commissioner of Indian Affairs quoted with exasperated approval the remark of a former attorney general of the United States that "there is nothing in the whole compass of our laws so anomalous, so hard to bring within any precise definition, or any logical and scientific arrangement of principles, as the relation in which the Indians stand towards this government and those of the States."[8]

The jury-rigging of federal policy toward the Indians that continued throughout the nineteenth century is evidence of just how imprecise and inadequate were the "principles" upon which generations of public officials attempted to construct a workable and codifiable relationship between white Americans and the Indians. The nature of the problem is suggested by the attorney general's own language: the official efforts to structure arrangements among people that could be called "precise," "logical," or "scientific"—the kinds of arrangements that, taken together, constitute "government"— were continually undermined by the persistent otherness of the Indians. The relationship between the U.S. government and the Indians was one that could not, from the perspective of those within the government, be clarified or stabilized through the imposition of an available discourse. There was no discourse that seemed able to put *Indians* and *government* together in any precise or logical relation except that of opposition.

The frustration expressed by the attorney general and the Commissioner of Indian Affairs is the result of their attempt to find what we might now call a master narrative, a discourse that would eliminate or submerge oppositions through new rhetorical arrangements and new definitions. Their need for the master narrative was widely shared not only by others who wrote about the "Indian question" in the nineteenth century but by those who wrote more generally about the evolution of culture and polity, as well as about the creation of policy, in America. What emerges from our rereading of some of this writing is the recognition that most of those who wrote shared the assumption that oppositions should and would be dissolved in the new nation, as the union became more perfect. Opposition ought to yield, in the natural course of things, to accommodation.

The yoking of oppositional or incompatible terms is characteristic of most of the rhetoric generated by "the Indian question" in the nineteenth century; the logical result of this kind of yoking is that the narratives in which the terms are contained almost inevitably conclude with the posing of either-or statements. No matter where the writer begins, and no matter what his or her sympathies, nineteenth-century analyses of "the Indian question" almost always end, as we shall see, at the virtually impassable stone wall of the choice between civilization and extinction for the Indians. The terms *civilization* and *extinction* are themselves rhetorically oppositional, in the sense that they are drawn from different discourses and therefore stand in a relation to each other that resists mediation or accommodation; the only way of linking the two terms within a rhetorically coherent statement—and therefore within an ideologically consistent discourse—is by use of the word *or*. And although the two terms are incompatible with each other, each invites combination with a series of other terms with which it is fully compatible; when one speaks of *civilization*, to take the most important example, one can also speak of *nations*, but when one speaks of *extinction*, the compatible terms are *tribe* or *race*. The stories of nations belong to the domain of modern history, while the stories of tribes and races belong more properly to the domain of ancient history (the tribes of Israel, the aboriginal races) or even natural history (the finny tribe, the feathered tribe).[9] The nations of the civilized world may rise and fall, but only tribes and races become extinct.

In his *History of the United States* (1840), George Bancroft raised the question of whether the Indians might have once belonged to nations and then have reverted to tribalism as the result of an extended period of migration. On the basis of his knowledge of Indian languages, Bancroft was able to refute the reversion hypothesis:

> It has been asked if our Indians were not the wrecks of more civilized nations. Their language refutes the hypothesis; every one of its forms is a witness that their ancestors were, like themselves, not yet disenthralled from nature. The character of each Indian language is one continued, universal, all-pervading synthesis. They to whom these languages were the mother tongue, were still in that earliest stage of intellectual culture where reflection has not begun.[10]

The fact that Bancroft was prepared to entertain the idea that Indian people once lived in "civilized nations," even if he was also prepared to reject the idea, suggests the binary nature of his conception of the possible modes of social and political organization. Either the Indians have always been tribal (and therefore uncivilized), or they once were organized into nations.

The nineteenth-century writing about the Indians that the following chapters examine constantly illustrates the difficulty white Americans had in conceiving of living Indian people as belonging to nations—either to their own Indian nations or to the new republican nation that white America was consciously constructing for itself. Indians are almost always referred to in this writing as belonging to race and tribe; eventually (at least by 1849), the Indians on reservations are even being referred to in official writing as "our colonized tribes."[11] This identification of Indian people as tribal is not in itself necessarily problematic as a form of ethnographic description. The problem is that the peculiarly unitarian character of American new-nation ideology, and of the rhetoric it produced, meant that tribalism was generally represented as antithetical to the entire project of nation-building.[12] The persistence of the notion that their tribal identity precluded Indian people from being or becoming members of a nation—that is, citizens—is reflected in the report of the Commissioner of Indian Affairs in 1856, who noted approvingly that one object of federal treaty-making with the Indians had been "the gradual abolition of the tribal character." (He also noted, in the context of discussing treaties and tribalism, that in the previous three and a half years the process of treaty-making had succeeded in removing from Indian control about 174 million acres of land, "either by the extinguishment of the original Indian title, or by the re-acquisition of lands granted to Indian tribes by former treaties. . . . ")[13] If tribal people could not qualify as citizens of a nation, neither should their claims to proprietorship of land within the geographical limits of the nation be considered valid.

In the chapters that follow, I have attempted first (Chapter 1) to restore the context of the public debates on the question of the Indians' place in the American nation and in the new American literature—debates that were both extensive and intensive—by surveying briefly the issues that were discussed in print, especially between 1830 and the middle of the 1850s. Then (Chapters 2, 3, and 4) I have reconsidered some nineteenth-century texts, including some very familiar ones, within that restored context in order to illustrate the ways in which they were responsive to the political, philosophical, and aesthetic issues raised by the Indian debates. My reconsideration of these texts has been grounded in two basic assumptions: first, that whether the American writer in this period wanted to address the question of the place of the Indians in national culture or to avoid it, there were few subjects that she or he could write about without in some way engaging it; and second, that as a result of that engagement, the American writer was, whether intentionally or not, contributing to the process of constructing a new-nation ideology, a process that both necessitated the removal or supplanting of inappropriate forms of discourse and justified the physical removal and supplanting of the Indians.

Although my purpose in Chapter 1 is to offer a general survey or representative sampling of contributions to the debates on the question of the incorporation of Indians into American public discourse, the succeeding chapters, in which I offer readings of specific literary texts, are not meant to constitute a survey. I have chosen instead to concentrate in these chapters on a few texts by a few writers, most of whom one would not ordinarily place on a list of American writers who addressed, or were even significantly influenced by, "the Indian question." All of these writers—Herman Melville, Catherine Sedgwick, Lydia Maria Child, Nathaniel Hawthorne, Margaret Fuller, Henry David Thoreau, and Francis Parkman—were New Englanders and therefore geographically distanced from the sites of actual physical conflict between Indians and white Americans. At the same time, because all were located at or near the center—both geographical and intellectual—of American literary production, the many implications of "the Indian question" were necessarily familiar and close to them and figured in their writing in ways that have not yet been closely examined.

In my own examination of these writers, I have concentrated on demonstrating the extent to which all of them were bound by the ideological and discursive limits imposed by the rhetoric of the civilization-or-extinction argument. I begin with Melville, and I give Melville the most space in the book because he is the one of the seven who is the most clearly aware of those limits; he is, therefore, also the only one who is visibly disturbed by a conviction that the American writer is legitimated only by acknowledging the limits and working within them. Of the seven, only Melville offers anything like a radical critique of the civilization-or-extinction argument (and its rhetoric), and even he is ultimately incapable of dislodging or replacing the models he is resisting. He can offer his critique only by populating his texts with significantly silent presences who, by their silence, call attention to their exclusion from American public discourse.

Melville, therefore, helps to define for us certain constraints within which the American writer was working, whether consciously or unconsciously, during much of the nineteenth century. He also helps us to recognize the complex and problematic relationship between the writing that was being produced in New England and the writing that was being generated on the American frontiers. The definition of that relationship was, as Melville seems to have known, deeply political in its nature and of critical importance to both the writer and the ordinary citizen, since it had everything to do with the larger definition of America as a nation and as a culture with claims to legitimacy.

In offering the survey that constitutes Chapter 1 (especially the first half of the chapter), I am going over some territory and summoning some arguments that will be familiar to many readers. I do so, at the risk of redundancy, because of my awareness that the territory I am recrossing, as familiar as it may be to some, has not yet been sufficiently defined as an appropriate site for locating an interpretation of canonical American texts. An important part of my purpose in this book is to argue that the history of white America's response to "the Indian question" is a history that *ought* to be familiar not just to specialists but to every serious and responsible reader of nineteenth-century American literature.

In the first chapter especially, but throughout the rest of the book as well, I am drawing on my reading of many other critics and interpreters whose work has made it possible for me to shape my own argument; my project is clearly grounded, as any project in literary or cultural criticism must be, in the work that has been done by others. Some of this work is acknowledged in the chapters that follow or in the notes; some of it is not. Among the critical books to which I am most indebted are several that, I am sure, will be as indispensable to the education of future writers on the subject of Indian-white relations as they were to me. These include Robert Berkhofer's *The*

White Man's Indian; Richard Drinnon's *Facing West*; Lesli€
The Return of the Vanishing American; Reginald Horsm;
and Manifest Destiny; Albert Keiser's *The Indian in Ame*
erature; Roy Harvey Pearce's *Savagism and Civilization*; ¿
ard Slotkin's *Regeneration Through Violence*.

These and other books provided me with essential inf
and with a series of theoretical perspectives that were use!
in situating my own argument; however, it was my rea(
different body of work—produced by Native American write
of them writing outside the academy—that most consisten
gized me as a critic and persuaded me of the necessity fc
sioning of the contexts within which the canonical literatu
nineteenth century was produced. The list of Native Ameri
ers whose work radically changed my thinking is a long one;
with Paula Gunn Allen, Vine Deloria, Louise Erdrich, Lind
Beatrice Medicine, Simon Ortiz, Wendy Rose, Leslie Marm
and Gerald Vizenor.

1 | Civilization or Extinction?

WHEN THE U.S. House of Representatives began its debates on the issue of the forced removal of the Cherokee Indians from the state of Georgia in 1831, Edward Everett of Massachusetts reminded his colleagues in the House of the crucial importance of the matter for the country as a whole: "I cannot disguise my impression, that it is the greatest question which ever came before Congress, short of the question of peace and war. It concerns not an individual, but entire communities of men, whose fate is wholly in our hands. . . . "[1] In that same year, when Chief Justice Marshall denied the Cherokees' request that the Supreme Court adjudicate their claims, he included in his written opinion a similar acknowledgment of the uniqueness of the issues that the removal question raised: "If courts were permitted to indulge their sympathies, a case better calculated to excite them can scarcely be imagined. . . . The condition of the Indians in relation to the United States is perhaps unlike that of any other two people in existence."[2] The sense of crisis that the removal question produced was not limited to the Congress and the courts; the fate of the Cherokees, and of other Indians east of the Mississippi, was the subject of intense debate in newspapers and magazines of every political persuasion. As a writer for the *American Quarterly Review* put it in early 1832, "Since the organization of our government, few

subjects have arisen which have agitated the public mind more violently or generally, than the controversy between the state of Georgia
and the Cherokee Indians."[3]

Frances Trollope was visiting Washington in 1831, making her
observations in preparation for writing *Domestic Manners of the
Americans*, while the removal debates were going on in Congress.
Her book records her reaction: "If the American character may be
judged by their conduct in this matter, they are most lamentably
deficient in every feeling of honour and integrity. It is among themselves, and from themselves, that I have heard the statements which
represent them as treacherous and false almost beyond belief in their
intercourse with the unhappy Indians." When Ralph Waldo Emerson
heard that the federal government had determined to remove the
Cherokees by force, he wrote to President Van Buren that "a crime
is being projected that confounds our understandings by its magni-
tude. . . . " The public sense of immediate crisis illustrated by these
reactions may have subsided after the forced removal of the Cherokees to the West in 1838, on what soon became known as the Trail
of Tears, but the public discussion of issues raised by the case continued, in various forms, throughout most of the rest of the nineteenth century, and its effects were still being felt at the end of the
century. In 1881, forty-three years after the Trail of Tears, Helen
Hunt Jackson wrote about the Cherokee removal with the same sense
of outrage that both Mrs. Trollope and Emerson had expressed: "In
the whole history of our Government's dealings with the Indian
tribes, there is no record so black as the record of its perfidy to [the
Cherokees]. There will come a time in the remote future when, to
the student of American history, it will seem well-nigh incredible."[4]

The passage of the Removal Act in 1830, which authorized the
federal government to exchange land west of the Mississippi for land
held by Indians living east of the river, and the Cherokees' subsequent refusal to trade their land and leave their homes, brought into
sudden, sharp focus a number of large and previously amorphous
issues and questions. These issues had certainly been in the air (and
on the page) since white settlers first made contact with the Indians
in North America, but the crisis of the 1830s forced the recognition

that attitudes that had been vaguely and randomly expressed before had now to be consolidated into a unified, practical, and defensible national policy. When white southerners asked the federal government to do something they construed as a fairly simple thing—that is, to force the Indians to obey whatever laws the states imposed on them, or remove the Indians from the states—they precipitated not only a major debate and a political crisis for the president, Andrew Jackson, but a widespread public reexamination of the terms in which the nation wished to define itself.

The case of the Cherokees drew greater public attention and initiated more serious debate than had previous encounters between the United States government and an Indian tribe for several reasons. In the first place, the federal government was for the first time considering giving official sanction to the forced removal of an entire Indian tribe from land it had occupied long before the whites began to make any permanent settlements there. In the second place, the Cherokees had been, for many years, quietly and successfully adapting the customs and practices of their white neighbors to their own purposes. By 1821 they had their own alphabet (invented by the mixed-blood George Guess, or Gist, now best known by his Indian name, Sequoyah), and not long after that, their own newspaper, the *Cherokee Phoenix*. By 1826 the tribe was estimated to own, among other things, 22,000 cattle, 7,600 horses, 2,948 plows, 1,277 black slaves, 10 sawmills, 31 grist mills, and 18 schools.[5] They adopted a written constitution in 1827 and established a bicameral legislature, and when the state of Georgia attempted to claim their tribal holdings as state land and replace their tribal law with state law, the Cherokees fought back by taking the matter to the federal courts and eventually to the Supreme Court. In short, the Cherokees were, by most American standards at the time, behaving like model citizens.

One additional reason that the case of the Cherokees drew so much attention was that it was a very public instance of the federal government's refusal to provide protection to an Indian tribe. The state of Georgia had begun systematically harassing the Cherokees through a series of repressive laws as soon as it was discovered that there was gold on Cherokee land. The tribe was forbidden by law to

mine its own gold, and the land held by the Cherokees was declared
to be state property; surveyors were sent in to divide the land into
tracts that could be apportioned to white Georgians through a state
lottery. The governing council of the tribe was forbidden to meet
except to ratify treaties. Furthermore, Indians were prohibited from
testifying against whites in the courts of the state, and any whites
who were living among the Indians—including missionaries—were
required to swear an oath of allegiance to the state of Georgia.

The Cherokees took their case to the U.S. Supreme Court twice,
in 1831 and 1832. The Court refused to rule in the first instance,
declaring the tribe a "domestic dependent nation" and therefore in-
eligible for the protection of the Court. The Court stood by that
ruling in 1832, but this time declared that the white citizens of Georgia had no right to enter Cherokee territory without the permission
of the tribe. This second decision seemed clearly a victory for the
Cherokees, but Georgia officials responded to the Court's mandate
by completely ignoring it. The harassing and dispossessing continued, with no interference from the federal government.

The violent conflicts between the Cherokees and the state of Georgia were finally "resolved" in 1835 through the signing of the Treaty
of New Echota, a document drawn up jointly by state and federal
officials, under the terms of which the Cherokees agreed to exchange
all of their land in the East for a payment of five million dollars and
joint interest in a tract of land in the Indian Territory established by
the Removal Act of 1830. When the treaty was first presented to the
elected representatives of the tribal council, they flatly refused to
sign. Undaunted, the white officials simply called together at New
Echota a group of Cherokees whom they knew to be in favor of
removal (estimates are that only between three hundred and five
hundred Cherokees out of a tribal population of seventeen thousand
were present), secured their signatures on the treaty, and rushed it
to Congress for ratification. The majority of the Cherokees disavowed
the treaty and continued their resistance to removal until 1838, when
federal troops were called in and the entire tribe, with the exception
of the few who managed to hide out in the hills, were forced to leave
their homes and farms and begin the long walk to the West.[6]

The question of whether the Cherokees ought to be removed forcibly from Georgia was, therefore, present to the American public and open to debate from at least the late 1820s until 1838. Both the proponents and the opponents of Cherokee removal recognized not only that an important precedent was likely to be set by the resolution of this conflict but that the international reputation of the fledgling American democracy had become one of the most crucial factors at stake in the case. In the course of his arguments before the Supreme Court, for example, the lawyer for the Cherokees declared that if the Court ruled in favor of the state of Georgia, then "our sun has gone down in treachery, blood and crime, in the face of the world; and, instead of being proud of our country, as heretofore, we may well call upon the rocks and mountains to hide our shame from earth and heaven."[7]

The proponents of removal, both within Georgia and elsewhere, clearly required a way of presenting their case that would allow them to counter the charge that in pursuing what many of their antagonists regarded as purely sectional interests, they were doing irreparable damage not only to the Cherokees but to the interests and, especially, the reputation of the country as a whole. Timothy Flint summarized the proremoval position at the end of his *Indian Wars of the West*, published in 1833. Having acknowledged that the issue of forced removal was "a vexed question, debated with intense interest, and no little asperity," Flint went on to cite with obvious approval the arguments of the proremoval forces:

> [T]he states, within whose limits [the Cherokees] reside, have perfect sovereignty in their hands, and an undoubted right either to compel their submission to their laws, or to remove them. They state, that it is impossible, that the Indians should exist, as an independent people, within the populous limits of the whites; that collisions, murders, escapes of fugitive slaves, and the operations of laws and usages so essentially different, as those of the white and red people, will forever keep alive between the contiguous parties, feuds, quarrels, and retaliations, which can never cease until one of the parties becomes extinct. They state, that commissioners, who have been sent to explore the country assigned to the Indians, who have already emigrated, find

them generally in healthy and fertile countries, satisfied with their condition, and advancing still more rapidly in agriculture, wealth, and civilization, than their brethren east of the Mississippi; and, that their removal will advance, instead of retarding these improvements.

Flint concluded his book with a projected vision of the utopian future awaiting the Indians in the West (a vision that seems to draw Flint away from summary of the arguments of others and into pure fancy):

[The] advocates of removal see the race perpetuated in opulence and peace in the fair prairies of the west. Here they are to grow up distinct red nations, with schools and churches, the anvil, the loom, and the plough—a sort of Arcadian race between our borders and the Rocky mountains, standing memorials of the kindness and good faith of our government.[8]

Flint's careful rendering of the case not only makes the forced removal of the Cherokees seem to be an act of national benevolence; it also makes forced removal seem the first logical step in the process of transforming a tribe of "red people" into a miniaturized (and for the time being, safely sequestered) version of the American nation.

Thomas Farnham, who traveled in 1839 across the Indian Territory set aside for the relocated tribes, returned to report that what he had seen confirmed the wisdom and prescience of the proremoval argument as Flint had outlined it. The Territory, Farnham reminded his readers, had been reserved through the benevolence of the federal government and only after the failure of the government's liberal efforts to "raise and ameliorate [the Indians'] condition in their old haunts within the precincts of the States," as a "suitable dwelling-place for a race of men which is passing from the savage to the civilized condition," a place where the Indians "might find a refuge from those influences which threaten the annihilation of their race." From his observations, Farnham was able to offer the cautiously optimistic conclusion that the policy of removal had begun to show encouraging signs of success in turning the relocated Indians into "reasoning, cultivated, and happy people." For Farnham, the next stage in the process of civilizing the Indians was clear: they were to be forced out of tribalism and trained in citizenship. To that end, Farnham wrote, the federal government should begin working to abolish traditional tribal forms of government, "making the rulers elective, establishing a form of government in each tribe, similar in department and duties to our State Governments, and uniting the tribes under a General Government, similar in powers and function to that at Washington."[9]

The public debates over the political expediency of removal were by no means silenced by the eventual forced resettlement of the Cherokees and other southeastern Indians in the West; the very presence of the Indians within the territory of the United States not only kept alive the sensitive issues associated with Indian removal but extended their implications beyond immediate practical and party questions and into other areas of American public life. Periodically, as the white population gradually expanded westward across or into Indian territory, the debates became intensified and localized: by the opening of the Oregon Trail, the Mexican War, the gold rush and the annexation of California, the Homestead Act, and so on. Throughout the period of this tremendous growth in the country, however, the *terms* of the public debate about the Indians remained essentially unchanged. The limits of the debate were largely defined by a few primal questions and the rhetoric they generated in response; once these were in place, they remained virtually fixed. And while the debate sustained itself through its own recirculated rhetoric, the Indians, of course, diminished in power and in numbers year by year.

The central question, the one on which most of the subsidiary questions depended, was articulated by William Bartram as early as 1791, in his introduction to the account of his travels in the southeastern United States. In his contacts with the Indians, Bartram wrote, he was especially concerned to determine for himself whether it was true that the Indians "were incapable of civilization," as their white neighbors alleged them to be:

> In consideration of this important subject it will be necessary to inquire, whether they were inclined to adopt the European modes of

civil society? Whether such a reformation could be obtained, without using coercive or violent means? And lastly, whether such a resolution would be productive of real benefit to them, and consequently beneficial to the public? I was satisfied in discovering that they were desirous of becoming united with us, in civil and religious society.[10]

While subsequent participants in the debate were usually not nearly so sanguine as Bartram about the future of the Indians, they did almost universally agree, overtly or tacitly, that every discussion of the subject must proceed from the single, all-important question with which Bartram begins: *Can the Indians be civilized?* And like Bartram, most writers who addressed the question assumed that the condition of being civilized had both a civil and a religious component (although there was some disagreement about which component had priority).[11]

Few of those who took for granted the necessity for civilizing the Indians ever explained (in print, anyway) precisely what they considered the attributes of the civilized person to be. Many seemed to find it sufficient, as did the traveler and ornithologist John Kirk Townsend, to offer "civilization" as the universal antidote for (and antithesis of) all that they found either offensive or inexplicable about the behavior of Indians. Townsend's contact with the western Indians in 1839 only confirmed the conviction with which he had set out from Philadelphia, that "nothing but the introduction of civilization, with its good and wholesome laws" could ever rescue the Indians from "the thralldom of vice, superstition, and indolence, to which they have so long submitted, and above which their energies have not enabled them to rise."[12]

A survey of the literature reveals that there were some specific assumptions about what constitutes "civilization" that were, if not universally agreed upon, at least never seriously contested in the literature. Foremost among them was the idea that any civilized society is founded on respect for private property. As the Commissioner of Indian Affairs put it in 1832, "The absence of the *meum* and *tuum* in the general community of possessions, which is the grand conservative principle of the social state, is a perpetuating cause of the *vis inertiae* of savage life." His successor reiterated the principle more

succinctly in his report for 1838: "Common property and civilization," he said flatly, "cannot co-exist." This belief that the Indians
could enter into civilized life only after they had learned the value
of acquiring and protecting private property dominated federal policy
toward the Indians throughout most of the century. The report of
the commissioner in 1888, for example, almost duplicated the language of the 1832 report: the Indian must, the report said, "be im-
bued with the exalting egotism of American civilization, so that he
will say 'I' instead of 'We,' and 'This is mine,' instead of 'This is
ours.' "[13] From an official standpoint, as long as the Indians did not
understand and practice the principles of private ownership and economic competition, they could not be considered eligible for inclusion
in civilized America.

The reflexive association of citizenship with respect for property
and with city-building is certainly not unique to the American experience. As Anthony Pagden has illustrated, the association was
made very clearly by Aristotle, who used the distinction between
those who inhabited cities and those who lived outside their limits
as the basis for his definition of the *barbaroi*, those who are less than
fully human:

> In the eyes of the Greeks, they themselves were the first, and the only
> true, city-dwellers. All the other races of men remained literally "out-
> side," where they lived in loose-knit hordes like the earliest survivors
> of Deucalion's flood, without laws or any knowledge of arts and crafts,
> and consequently alien to any form of virtue, for virtue can only be
> practised within the *polis*.[14]

Two other of the requirements for civilization on which there was
widespread agreement were conversion to Christianity and the adoption of the English language, although the two were seen as so closely
related that they were frequently merged into a single requirement.
Native languages, it was generally agreed, were limited by their
primitive inflexibility: they had no alphabets and thus could not be
written, and they were so rooted in the physical world that they did
not allow for the abstract thinking and logical reasoning necessary
for comprehending the principles of either democratic capitalism or

Christianity. White observers consistently concluded that because of the limitations of his or her language, the most complex intellectual maneuver any Indian (of whatever language group) could manage was the construction of a simple metaphor, or occasionally an analogy; the Indian could not speculate about things that have no visible form, nor comprehend notional ideas. The Indian agent Jedediah Morse, writing a report of his experiences for the secretary of war, concluded that there was no reason to try to preserve any Indian languages, except as specimens and curiosities. "As fast as possible," Morse wrote in 1822,

> let Indians forget their own languages, in which nothing is written, and nothing of course can be preserved, and learn ours, which will at once open to them the whole field of every kind of useful knowledge. ... Let the Indians of our country be taught to read and speak the English language, and it will effect more towards civilizing and christianizing them than all human means besides.[15]

Morse's attitude toward native languages quickly became part of official government policy, as the Commissioners of Indian Affairs throughout the nineteenth century reiterated the necessity for establishing schools in which priority would be given to replacing the native languages of Indian children with English. Thomas Farnham restated Morse's position in 1843 when he wrote that "the most successful means of civilizing [the Indians'] mental state, is to teach them a language which is filled with the learning, sciences, and the religion which has civilized Europe, that they may enter at once, and with the fullest rigour into the immense harvests of knowledge and virtue which past ages and superior races have prepared for them."[16]

The fundamental question of the Indians' capacity for assimilation into white American society was usually contextualized by the almost universally shared assumption that there were only two options for the Indians: to become *civilized*, or to become *extinct*. This civilization/extinction dichotomy was freely accepted and just as freely manipulated by both sides in the controversy over the removal of the Indians to the West. Some of the official proponents of removal, like the first Commissioner of Indian Affairs, Thomas McKenney, argued that moving the Indians west was actually the most humane and beneficent policy the government could adopt, since the only way to accomplish the civilizing of the Indians, and thus assure that they did not become extinct, was to move them beyond the reach of unscrupulous whites who wished to do them harm. This argument was also the one advanced by the southern politicians who finally carried the day when the removal bill came to a vote in Congress. Although it was clear that local Georgia officials had very practical reasons for wanting to move the Indians out of the state (the recent discovery of gold on Cherokee land, for example, the refusal of the tribe to cede any more land to the state, and the suspicion that the Cherokees were harboring runaway slaves), the position taken by the proremoval forces in public debate was that the reasons for removal were completely humanitarian: on their new land in the West, protected by a paternal and benign federal government, the Indians could gradually be prepared for eventual citizenship. Left on their own to compete with superior whites for territory in the East, the argument went, they were certain to be decimated.

The proremoval argument had the appeal of a quick fix to pressing problems and was therefore difficult to counter. Even the early opponents of removal, such as Lewis Cass (then governor of the Michigan Territory), were generally more skeptical about the chances for success with their plans than were the proponents of removal. Cass argued in 1826 that while the Indians might be victimized by whites if they remained in the East, they were sure to kill each other if forced to live together in the West, given their "war-like" nature. He proposed that the most reasonable way to "preserve [Indians] from decline and extinction" was for the federal government to strengthen and expand the policies already in place, providing more Indian agents and stricter enforcement of trade regulations, and giving stronger encouragement to the Indians to "hold separate property." Having spelled out his practical proposals, however, Cass could only throw up his hands and conclude that "after all this, we should leave their fate to the common God of the white man and the Indian."[17]

Those participants in the public debate who were not directly responsible for creating and defending public policy—that is, the writers who were not also politicians or government employees—were free to be somewhat more outspoken on the issues. Among them were some who considered removal a waste of money and effort, since they saw no possibility of saving the Indians, whether they were moved west or not. These hard-liners were the most vocal in affirming that extinction was the only alternative to civilization, and since they found the Indians incapable of becoming civilized by their very nature, they predicted for them a quick removal not just from the areas of white settlement but from history itself. A writer for the *North American Review* in 1826 concluded, tersely, that "a community of *civilized Indians* is an anomaly that never has existed, nor do we believe it ever will exist." As this writer saw it, the fate of the Indians was, inevitably, to join the other races who had already "disappeared before the march of civilization."[18] In 1830 the *American Quarterly Review* carried an article responding to the passage of the removal bill and predicting the failure of the policy, on the grounds that it only delayed the inevitable: "It has been decreed by Providence, that the civilized and the savage man never shall live for any length of time on the same soil. Either the one or the other must be blotted out of existence."[19] In 1838, the year the Cherokees were forced onto the Trail of Tears, the *North American Review* ran an essay that included this peroration:

> The moment the new world was discovered, the doom of the savage races who inhabited it was sealed; they must either conform to the institutions of the Europeans, or disappear from the face of the earth. . . . Barbarism and civilization were set up, face to face, and one or the other must fall in the encounter. The history of two hundred years is a perpetual commentary upon this text.[20]

There were, of course, other writers who were much more inclined to be sympathetic to the Indians and who were evidently genuinely distressed by what was happening to them; yet in many cases their sympathy led only to a conflicted or ambivalent response to the question of whether the Indians could be saved through an effort at civilizing them. Charles Fenno Hoffman, for example, whose travel letters from the midwestern frontier were first published in the New York *American* in the winter of 1833–1834, was consistently admiring of the Indians he encountered and angered by the results of the removal policy; nevertheless, Hoffman still wrote that "Providence seems to have designed that this mysterious race should not continue upon the earth. . . . You may talk of civilizing them,—but that, too, is impossible. . . . " For Hoffman, the "American savage" was "the genuine child of nature—the untamed,—the untameable."[21]

When Ralph Waldo Emerson lectured to his fellow citizens of Concord in 1835 on the history of their town, he addressed the subject of seventeenth-century relations between Indians and whites in ways that suggest that his reaction to the contemporary crisis in Indian-white relations was even more ambivalent than Hoffman's. Emerson spoke with approval of the efforts of the early settlers to civilize and christianize the Indians, but he also spoke of the sad failure of the whites to accomplish their objectives. The reasons for the failure, according to Emerson, were attributable in part to the "envenomed prejudice" of many of the whites but also in part to the fact that the Indians seemed incapable of giving up their nomadic hunting habits, settling into towns, and learning how to be Christian citizens: "The man of the woods might well draw on himself the compassion of the planters. His erect and perfect form, though disclosing some irregular virtues, was found joined to a dwindled soul. . . . Those who dwelled by ponds and rivers had some tincture of civility, but the hunters of the tribe were found intractable at catechism." Emerson especially praised the efforts of the missionary John Eliot to convert the Indians to Christianity. When Eliot preached, according to Emerson, the Indians listened and were changed: "There under the rubbish and ruins of barbarous life, the human heart heard the voice of love, and awoke from a sleep." And yet, Emerson continued, a few compassionate whites like Eliot were not enough to save the Indians of New England:

We, who see in the squalid remnants of the twenty tribes of Massachusetts, the final failure of this benevolent enterprise, can hardly learn without emotion, the earnestness with which the most sensible individuals of the copper race held on to the new hope they had conceived, of being elevated to equality with their civilized brother.

In this lecture Emerson expressed his pity for the Indians and accused the whites of a lack of charity toward them, but he still concluded that the seventeenth-century "benevolent enterprise," the earliest effort to settle the "Indian question" by demonstrating that the Indians could be civilized and christianized, had been a complete failure.[22]

By the end of the 1830s, removal had become an accomplished fact, and it had become clear that the territorial contest between Indians and whites would continue to be an unequal one. The U.S. government, having taken a critical step in entertaining arguments for the forced removal of the Cherokees, subsequently used military force to subdue and remove the rebellious Sauks and Foxes in Illinois, under Black Hawk, and the Seminoles in Florida. Black Hawk's resistance (in 1832) was put down fairly quickly, but to the apparent surprise of almost everyone, the subduing of the Seminoles turned out to be a long and costly process. The resistance of the Seminoles resulted in a guerilla war, carried on in the swamps of Florida where the Indians, who were on familiar turf, had sufficient advantage over the more numerous and better-armed white troops to keep the war going for seven years, from 1835 to 1842. The *North American Review* predicted, in the sixth year of the war, that it would be regarded by posterity as "one of the most successful struggles which history exhibits, of a barbarous, weak, and almost destitute people, with a civilized, strong, and abundantly provided nation."[23] Later estimates, after the last of the Seminoles were finally removed, put the total cost of the war to the U.S. government at approximately fifteen hundred soldiers and twenty million dollars. Most of the remaining eastern Indians, already much reduced in numbers, were persuaded to emigrate without significant resistance. By 1838, according to the best estimates of the commissioner of Indian Affairs, a total of 81,000 Indians had been removed to land west of the Mississippi, leaving only 26,700 in the East.[24]

As the Indians succumbed to the political and military power of the whites, so even those white writers who were most sympathetic to the Indians seem to have succumbed to the rhetoric of the hard-line expansionists. William L. Stone, who wrote two generally ad-miring Indian biographies (of the Mohawk chief Joseph Brant and the Seneca spokesman Red-Jacket), ended his 1841 book on Red-Jacket by asking rhetorically whether any of the North American Indians were "eventually to yield to the influences and usages of civilization, and thus to be rescued from extinction?" Stone's brief examination of the question led him to "the sad conclusion, that their destiny is to be,—EXTINCTION!"[25] In another book published in 1841, George Catlin's *Letters and Notes on the Manners, Customs, and Conditions of the North American Indians*, Catlin argued that his visits to the Indians beyond the frontier had convinced him that the term "savage" had been misapplied to the Indians by prejudiced whites; the Indians in their natural state were in fact, Catlin argued, "a truly lofty and noble race." In spite of his admiration for the Indians he encountered, Catlin could only fall back into the old rhet-oric—and thus into contradiction—when addressing the question of what was to become of the Indians of the West. While insisting that "they are *'doomed'* and must perish," Catlin held out the faint hope that a few of the Indians might be rescued by the right kind of missionaries, who would "be able to solve to the world the perplexing enigma, by presenting a nation of savages, civilized and christianized (and consequently *saved*), in the heart of the American wilderness."[26]

Catlin's belief that the best hope for the Indians lay with the white missionaries, who might succeed in saving at least some of the Indians from extinction by making Christian citizens of them, was shared by many of the missionaries themselves. In 1838 the Rev-erend Samuel Parker published an account of his travels to the West Coast as an emissary of the American Board of Commissioners for Foreign Missions; Parker's instructions from the board were "to as-certain, by personal observation, the condition and character of the Indian nations and tribes, and the facilities for introducing the gospel and civilization among them." His report indicates that Parker under-stood his ultimate objective to be that of determining whether an intensified missionary effort (and therefore increased financial con-

tributions to missions) could in fact rescue the Indians from annihilation and convert them into productive Americans:

> The future condition of this noble race of men is a subject of interesting
> enquiry to many others as well as myself. Whether the Indians are
> to pass away before the increasing power and numbers of white men;
> or whether enlightened and improved by their philanthropy, they shall
> arise in the scale of human existence is a question, which at the present
> time is attracting attention and inviting investigation.

For Parker, the civilizing of the Indians was dependent on their will-
ingness to give up hunting in favor of farming, a conversion that he
saw as impossible "until their minds are enlightened by divine
truth." Not surprisingly, Parker's conclusions about the missionaries' ability to raise the Indians to the level of citizens were thoroughly
optimistic: "Why shall not a redeeming influence be exerted to bring
the Indians to an elevated condition, to which their independent and
ambitious dispositions aspire, and to which God, as a part of the
family of man, designed them?"[27]

As the debate about the Indians continued through the years of
westward expansion by white settlers, the essential shape of the argument changed very little; the major changes occurred only in the
tone of the rhetoric. Although the idea that the Indians were heading
rapidly toward extinction was never seriously disputed, there were
many who publicly lamented (in more and more sentimental ways)
the disappearance of the Indians, and many others who found in their
demise a reason for renewed national confidence and optimism. The
Democratic Review, for example, carried an essay in 1842 in which
the writer found it "melancholy to reflect that, judging from the
past, no future event seems more certain than the speedy disappearance of the American aboriginal race."[28] Two years later the same
journal published a much more cheerfully optimistic article describing the history of white-Indian relations as a conflict between "the
alpha and omega of the ethnological chain." If white Anglo-Saxons
had evidenced their superiority from the beginning, it was because
"Christianity was superior to paganism; industry to idleness; agriculture to hunting; letters to hieroglyphics; truth to error. Here lies

the true secret of the Red Man's decline." There was nothing to regret about moving the Indians out of the way or about anticipating their ultimate disappearance, this writer observed, since the whites were simply obeying their racial instinct to "carry on man to his highest destiny."[29]

The fated disappearance of the Indians, whether for good or for ill, became an increasingly popular subject in the literary magazines and in schoolbooks between 1830 and 1860. One of the most popular inclusions in school readers of the period, for example, was a speech given by Justice Joseph Story on the future of the Indians. "What can be more melancholy," Story asked, "than their history? By a law of nature they seem destined to a slow but sure extinction. Everywhere at the approach of the white man they fade away." Many of the school readers also included poems about the Indians, most of them laments over the "melancholy" destiny of the "red man."[30] The adult equivalent of the school readers, the literary magazines, similarly began to publish more and more sentimental eulogies for the vanishing Indian. (The dying Indian had already become established as a popular figure in sentimental poetry in both England and America by the late eighteenth century; however, these earlier representations tended to emphasize the Indians' stoical endurance of suffering, whereas the later efforts, significantly, more often presented the individual Indian's death as a synechdoche for the extinction of all North American Indians.)[31] Typical of this kind of writing is a piece called "The Last of the Tribes," published in the *Southern Literary Messenger* for 1845. The writer observes that the Plains Indians have begun to "vanish away before the white man," and predicts that soon the movement of whites to the Pacific coast will necessitate a similar fate for the Indians west of the Rockies. The whites have, he notes, already begun their push into Oregon, "and before their onward march, the tribes of the red men will doubtless wither and fade away, as if by some resistless ordinance of nature." The real purpose of this rather cheerful assertion of the naturalness of the Indians' extermination is to introduce a long poem, "The Lament of the Last of the Tribes," in which a lonely Indian stands on the shore of the Pacific Ocean and weeps over the fate of his people, "Sinking, wearied, in their grave, / By the blue Pacific's wave!" The sentimentality of the poem seems intended to complement the firm assertiveness of the prose introduction, assuring the reader that the expansionist who accepts the necessary extinction of the Indians may also be a man of deep feeling.[32]

The idea that the Indians were fated to give way to white American progress was given added impetus, and the semblance of a scientific basis, by the midcentury interest in the new discipline of ethnology; in the United States the methods of the ethnologists were welcomed by both the advocates of black slavery and by those who looked forward to the extinction of the Indian. The earlier American ethnologists, men like Samuel George Morton and Charles Caldwell, relied primarily on phrenological measurements and scriptural evidence to demonstrate the superiority of the white race over all the darker races.[33] In 1848, however, Frederick William Van Amringe published *An Investigation of the Theories of the Natural History of Man*, in which he used what he saw as the irrefutable evidence of documented history to demonstrate that white people were the only ones capable of continued improvement. Van Amringe divided humanity into four races—white, yellow, red, and black—and assessed the capacity of each to progress beyond what he defined as its present social and intellectual condition. His conclusion, which he acknowledged to be a "melancholy" one, was that "the dark races are doomed to extinction by the gradual increase of the white race, by a process similar to that which is now fast extinguishing the aborigines of North America." The publication of the book was greeted by a long and enthusiastically laudatory article in the *Democratic Review*.[34]

Not surprisingly, the theory that the white race was genetically destined to inherit the earth (especially the North American portion of the earth) found strong support in the American South, since the white supremacy argument allowed southerners to justify both keeping their slaves and getting rid of "their" Indians. Among the southern writers whose work most consistently exploited the arguments for white supremacy was William Gilmore Simms. While Simms was given to creating sympathetic Indian heroes and heroines of the "noble-savage" sort in his fiction, he clearly was not prepared to grant the Indians a place in contemporary American culture; in fact, Simms's vision of the national character, and of the prospects for the country's future, were predicated on his conviction that the Indians had been safely sequestered in the historical past. He summarized his position very clearly at the beginning of his 1856 novel, *Charlemont: or, the Pride of the Village*. The novel is set in Kentucky, and Simms notes that the state is no longer "the bloody ground" of conflict between whites and Indians:

> The savage had disappeared from its green forests for ever, and no longer profaned with slaughter, and his unholy whoop of death, its broad and beautiful abodes. A newer race had succeeded; and the wilderness, fulfilling the better destinies of earth, had begun to blossom like the rose. . . . High and becoming purposes of social life and thoughtful enterprise superseded that eating and painful decay, which has terminated in the annihilation of the red man. . . . [35]

Simms dedicated *Charlemont* to Judge James Hall, the popular writer of western stories, much of whose own fiction is based on the same complacent assumption that, as Hall puts it in one story, "the savage must retire before civilized man."[36]

Simms was thus able to draw on the images of savage life (and their associated rhetoric) that were already in place and put them to use in the "civilized" discourse of the white supremacist, whose real purpose was to celebrate the moral and political destiny of white America and to affirm that the suppression of other races, through slavery or "annihilation," was part of a natural process of evolution. Somewhat more surprisingly, the stereotypical images of savage life were also brought into the midcentury debates on another important social and political issue, the question of the rights of women. As in the case of the arguments about race, the discourse generated by "the woman question" established the kinds of binary categories that were rhetorically consistent with the distinctions between savagery and civilization and that therefore invited a rhetorical merging of the two issues. In 1836 Caleb Cushing argued in the *North American Review* that white women in America were better off than any other women in history and ought to be content with their social position, since

they alone had been given the freedom to rule "the domain of the
moral affections, the empire of the heart" and to share in "the co-
equal sovereignty of intellect, taste and social refinement. . . . " Cushing contrasted the status of women in white, Christian society to that
of Indian women, whom he (like many other whites) saw as forced
by Indian custom to be slaves to their husbands: "Woman is the
humble slave of his pleasure, the handmaid of his daily wants, his
laborious drudge of the field, the household, and the journey, con-
signed to toil and subservience, while he, the proud lord of creation,
aspires exclusively to the stirring chances of the chase, or the yet
nobler game of war."[37] Lady Sydney Morgan, on the other hand,
offered (in 1840) a similar image of the Indian woman's life to argue
that, no matter how primitive Indian men might be, no matter how
"sensual, slothful, sullen, and saturnine," they still illustrated the
universal male instinct to assert their dominance over women. For
Lady Morgan, the problem with the Red Man was not so much that
he was Red as that he was Man:

> The brief and bloody story of the Red Man of the northern hemi-
> sphere, the destroyer and the destroyed, is thus soon told. Yet he, too,
> all savage as he is, has a seeming consciousness of some divine law,
> authorizing him to assume a despotic supremacy over the female of
> his species. Wallowing in indolence, when not wallowing in blood, he
> leaves to the woman, his servant, all the labour, forethought, and
> ingenuity, necessary for the wants of his savage interior. . . . [38]

Even Margaret Fuller and Mary Eastman, both of whom were deeply
sympathetic with the plight of American Indians and especially interested in observing the lives of Indian women, still fell easily into
what now seem surprisingly naive distinctions between civilized and
savage women. Fuller wrote in 1843 that "it is impossible to look
upon the Indian women, without feeling that they *do* occupy a lower
place than women among the nations of European civilization." And
Eastman, in the course of her otherwise clear-eyed account of Dakota
Sioux culture (published in 1849), remarks that "a degraded state of
woman is universally characteristic of savage life, as her elevated
influence in civilized society is the conspicuous standard of moral and
social virtue."[39]

This assimilation of the generic Indian woman into the arguments over the status of white women in America was made possible by the earlier arguments over whether or not the Indians themselves could be assimilated into the white culture. The fact that the figure of the Indian could be brought in so handily when the point of the argument was to contrast higher with lower, superior with inferior, progressive with regressive, suggests, among other things, how widely accepted were the dichotomies that characterized the discourse of the debates on "the Indian question."

The debates about official policy toward the Indians were by no means settled by midcentury, but they had begun to be muted (or, as I have suggested, subsumed) by newer and louder debates—especially those over slavery and the organization of new states and territories. The Commissioner of Indian Affairs in 1851 was still using the obligatory rhetoric about civilizing the Indians in the West before they became extinct and still insisting that "the great question, How shall the Indians be civilized? yet remains without a satisfactory answer."[40] His primary concern now, however, was to move the Indians out of the way of the flood of emigrating whites. He recommended "the removal of a few tribes" who were already placed on western reservations in order to "throw open a wide extent of country for the spread of our population westward."[41] By this time he did not need to justify his recommendations: the Indians were, at this point, removable at will. The earlier political expedient of moving the Indians to the West, for the ostensible purpose of saving their lives, only made it easier for the federal government to justify whatever subsequent removals were called for. In 1867, when the Cheyennes and Arapahoes resisted the building of the Union Pacific Railroad through their midwestern hunting grounds, the only question for federal officials was not *whether* to move the Indians out of the way but only *how* to move them most efficiently. The alternatives were set out clearly by one of the agents sent from Washington to survey the situation, General William Tecumseh Sherman, in his report to the secretary of war:

> My opinion is, if fifty Indians are allowed to remain between the Arkansas and the Platte we will have to guard every stage station,

every train, and all railroad working parties. In other words, fifty hostile Indians will checkmate three thousand soldiers. Rather get them out as soon as possible, and it makes little difference whether they be coaxed out by Indian commissioners or killed.[42]

At the same time that many white Americans were arguing about the capacity of the Indians to participate in the developing political and social life of the country, many—especially in the east—were also arguing about the relevance of the Indian presence in North America to the development of a national literature. The specific vocabulary of this literary debate on the "Indian question" necessarily differed from that of the civic debate, but its rhetorical strategies and boundaries did not; the nature of the questions asked and the limits imposed by those questions were essentially the same in both cases. The perpetual question in both debates, the one generally taken to be irreducible, was whether the Indians were capable of assimilation into the white culture of America: in one case as inhabitants of its states, and in the other as inhabitants of its emerging, civilized literature. The crucial question, that is, was still whether or not the Indians could be *civilized*. And in both debates, the only alternative imagined for the Indians was extinction: through literal death, or through banishment from the version of history that the culture chose to preserve in its literature. It is not surprising that the arguments about the place of the Indians in American literature produced intense, frequently angry reactions, since what was really at issue in this debate was the image of itself that America was in the process of sanctioning and offering to the rest of the world. As Cathy Davidson has pointed out, "For the social spokespersons of the new Republic, an aberrant form of literary culture *equaled* an aberration in the very design of America."[43]

Although William Gilmore Simms had, as we have seen, consistently declared the Indians necessarily irrelevant to the future of American *society*, his was at the same time one of the strongest voices to insist on the peculiar relevance of the Indians to the future of American *literature*. In both his fiction and his criticism, Simms did his best to keep before the public his convictions about the need for a national literature and his ideas about where the sources of that

literature were to be found. He was fully persuaded that the United
States would never achieve its complete independence from Britain,
or be recognized abroad as a mature civilization, until it began to
produce an indigenous literature that was taken seriously by Americans and, especially, by Europeans. As long as American writers
continued to imitate the English, Simms argued, they would remain
the objects of continued contempt from the literary establishment of
the country that Simms called America's "imperious mother."
Simms was frankly ambitious in his aims: he wanted a national
literature that would compete not only with Walter Scott and Shakespeare but with Homer and Virgil as well. In his essays (collected
and published as *Views and Reviews in American Literature, History
and Fiction* in 1846), he argued that the time was right for America
to accomplish its national mission, "a mission commensurate to the
extent of our country"; it was time, that is, for America to find and
acknowledge its own geniuses, who could see in the history of the
country "a body of crude material, virgin and fertile," waiting to
give birth to an epic literature.[44]

For Simms, the Indians provided a critical portion of the material
available to the American genius; they were, after all, the most obvious resource the American writers had that the English did not.
They were our Gauls and our Goths, Simms explained, waiting for
"the future Homer" to make them "immortal on the lips of eternal
song." Simms went so far in his enthusiasm for exploiting the Indians in the cause of American cultural independence from England
as to argue that the Indians themselves might well have produced
their own Homers and preserved their own cultural resources, had
the English colonists only dealt with them more forcefully:

> Had these English settlements been such as a mighty nation should
> have sent forth—had the colonies been such as issued from the fruitful
> ports of Carthage,—thirty thousand at a time, as were sent out by
> Hanno,—what would have been the effect upon the destinies of the
> red men of America. They would have been rescued from themselves
> and preserved,—a mighty nation, full of fire, of talent, of all the
> materials which ensure long life to the genius and to the eminence of
> a race.[45]

However, since the English bungled the job as colonizers through their lack of aggression, and since the Indians were therefore, as Simms believed, becoming extinct without having made any use of their own rich materials, it was left to white American writers to take the fullest possible advantage of whatever Indian mythology and history they could still retrieve.

The most controversial part of Simms's argument was his insistence that part of the white writer's obligation was to *change* the Indian materials—even the relatively few known facts of Indian history—to make them appropriate subjects for the epic literature of America. Other writers before Simms had protested that accuracy was not a primary consideration in treating Indian materials. Robert Strange, for example, in the introduction to his 1839 novel *Eoneguski, or The Cherokee Chief*, had pointed out that if "truth and accuracy" were a requirement for all writing, then "Homer and Milton would never . . . have become the standards of taste and models of poetic excellence for all generations."[46] But Simms was much more outspoken than Strange in arguing that the American Homer would *need* to revise the Indian matter, the raw material, to make it usable for the great New World epic. The Indian matter, that is, needed to be "civilized" by the white writer.

In offering this argument, Simms was to some extent attempting to sidestep those critics who had already objected to the sheer rawness of the Indian material. In an 1830 review of John Tanner's captivity narrative in the *American Quarterly Review*, for example, the reviewer found Tanner's accounts of the day-to-day life of the Indians of the Northwest Territory so revolting that he could not bring himself to choose any excerpts to include in his review: "we found the task so sickening that we threw it up in disgust, and we have too high an opinion of the moral taste of our community, not to be convinced that they will approve of our determination."[47] A reviewer for the *New-England Magazine* in 1834 found that the American public had already been "nauseated . . . for four or five years with Indian novels, Indian stories, and travels in Indian country," and a year later in the same journal a weary-voiced reviewer of Judge Hall's *Tales of the Border* noted that "Indian murder or speech is the heaviest drug in the market."[48] Simms was therefore careful to insist that the American genius required a transforming aesthetic imagination, so that he could apply to the native materials "some softening lights, some subduing touches" in order to give them "coherence and effect" and, especially, a "higher moral tone." Simms was able to justify such fiddling with the record of the past by a simple mandate: "The truth is . . . the chief value of history consists in its proper employment for the purposes of art!"[49]

Interestingly, Simms's attitudes toward the Indians, although founded ultimately on the principle of white supremacy, did not preclude the possibility of intermarriage between whites and Indians. He speculated that had this practice begun early enough, the result would have been an infusion of the best qualities of the Indian character—pride and independence—into the blood of the early colonists, a result that might well have hastened the break with England and the formation of a distinctively American character.[50] The intermarriage of whites and Indians had been suggested by others before Simms; Jedediah Morse, for example, in his 1822 report to the secretary of war, urged that the government give first priority to educating and christianizing Indian women, to fit them for marriage with white men.[51] A writer for the *North American Review* in 1826 agreed that intermarriage was one effective way of solving the Indian problem, since the superior blood would surely dominate, with the result that "the red skin will become white."[52] The subject became shocking only when the envisioned marriage was specified as taking place between a white woman and an Indian man. A reviewer of Lydia Maria Child's *Hobomok* (1824), for example, while praising the novel in general ways, found its portrayal of the white heroine's marriage to an Indian "not only unnatural, but revolting . . . to every feeling of delicacy in man or woman."[53]

In retrospect, all of these attitudes toward intermarriage can be seen to be thoroughly consistent with the terms of Simms's argument for incorporating the Indians into the literature of America; just as the real Indians could be gradually transformed into white people through the marriage of properly educated Indian women to white men, so the history of the Indians, properly revised, could become the "body of crude material, virgin and fertile" Simms spoke of, made available for "all the maternal uses which grow naturally from the embrace of the prolific [white male] genius."[54]

Although Simms's high visibility and the sheer amount of writing he produced made his name closely associated with the argument for a national literature, he was certainly not the first to raise the issue, nor was he the only one to place the Indians at the center of the argument. (The *Knickerbocker Magazine* complained in 1847 that "it was thought for some time that we could have no 'American literature' unless our writers infused a large proportion of Indian character into all their works; so that we came to have aboriginal ingredients in all our indigenous intellectual food. . . . "[55]) Simms's great ally in the cause of literary nationalism, Cornelius Mathews, even produced a novel (*Behemoth: A Legend of the Mound-Builders*, 1846) in which he attempted to make *pre*historic America "subservient to the purposes of imagination." Mathews's plot pits the behemoth against the Mound Builders, "the great race that preceded the red men as the possessors of our continent," in what was clearly meant to be an epic struggle.[56]

Nationalists like Simms and Mathews had before them the inspiring early example of Washington Irving, whose *Sketchbook of Geoffrey Crayon, Esq.* (1819) was sufficiently well received in England to be strongly encouraging to those who were looking for evidence that American writers were capable of competing with, and eventually supplanting, British writers. Significantly, in putting together an edition of the *Sketchbook* for an English publisher (1820), Irving pulled out of his files two essays that he had not included in the American edition—one on the Wampanoag chief known as King Philip and another called "Traits of Indian Character." By inserting these two into the new edition, Irving thus reinforced for his English audience the Americanness of his collection of literary sketches and his own claim, as an American writer, to what he called the "wonderfully striking and sublime" material provided by the history of the Indians.[57]

The argument for incorporating the Indians into American literature was also advanced by the fiction-writer Caroline Kirkland, although her name has never been as closely associated with literary nationalism as have the names of Simms, Mathews, and Irving— perhaps because she was less outspoken than the men or because she entered the fray relatively late, or perhaps simply because of her gender. In her preface to Mary Eastman's *Dahcotah: Or, Life and Legends of the Sioux*, published in 1849, Kirkland noted the irony of many American writers' reluctance to use Indian materials: the Americans were frustrated by charges of imitativeness and were desperately looking for original subjects, Kirkland wrote, yet they persisted in ignoring the one American subject that was perceived as most striking and "poetical" to those "eyes across the water" that the Americans were so intent on impressing. In examining the question of *why* most American writers stubbornly avoided the Indians, who embodied "all the distinct and characteristic poetic material to which we, as Americans, have an unquestioned right," Kirkland arrived at the conclusion that the reasons could be traced to an unacknowledged moral (and political) cowardice. The Indians, she found, were still geographically and psychologically too close to white Americans for comfort:

> To look upon the Indian with much regard, even in the light of literary material, would be inconvenient; for the moment we recognize in him a mind, a heart, a soul,—the recollection of the position in which we stand towards him becomes thorny, and we begin dimly to remember certain duties belonging to our Christian profession, which we have sadly neglected with regard to the sons of the forest, whom we have driven before us just as fast as we have required or desired their land.

For Kirkland, preserving what she called the "Iliad material" offered by the Indians was as much a moral duty for white Americans—one obligation of the literate and powerful to the illiterate and powerless—as it was an opportunity to escape the cultural domination of the English. The Indians, she concluded, "live poetry; it should be ours to write it out for them."[58] If white America did not have a clear right to appropriate Indian land, it did at least have the right to appropriate *Indianness* and use it in the service of white America's claims to cultural independence and legitimacy.

In the periodical literature of the 1830s, 1840s, and early 1850s, the question of whether American writers ought to devote themselves to identifiably American themes appears, over and over, in the context of reviews of works about the Indians. On one side of the argument among critics and reviewers were those who were inclined (like Simms) to be sympathetic to any attempts to represent Indians in fiction and poetry, on the grounds that such attempts helped to increase the corpus of genuinely national literature. A reviewer for the *North American Review* in 1828, for example, praised Catherine Sedgwick's novel *Hope Leslie* because of its successful use of colonial materials to produce work of "purely national manufacture, and original patterns." The reviewer had to admit that Sedgwick's portrait of her Indian heroine, Magawisca, failed in verisimilitude, but defended Sedgwick by pointing out that her intent was only to create "a possible Indian," not a likely one.[59] In 1834 the *New-England Magazine* carried a review of William Stone's *Tales and Sketches* in which the reviewer noted approvingly the recent efforts of several "clever writers" (including Sedgwick) to contribute to the formation of a national literature by writing about the Indians, "a people who never thought that they had any thing peculiar in manner and habit." The reviewer singled out Stone as the best of these writers, on the grounds that he "has read more directly the characters of Indians and New-England men, than any of his predecessors, and has portrayed them with spirit. . . ."[60] In a review of W. H. C. Hosmer's long poem *Yonnodio: or, Warriors of the Genessee!* that appeared in the *Southern Literary Messenger* in 1845, the writer praised Hosmer's effort (while managing to say very little about the poem itself) because "we like to see a spirit of nationality pervading the effusions of the bard," and "the subject of Yonnodio is *American*. The burden of the song is of a race which . . . had their birth, and still have their homes exclusively on this continent."[61]

On the other side of the argument were those critics who objected in general to the representation of Indians in literature on the grounds that the mythologized or "possible" Indian was a lie and the more realistic portraits of Indians were, simply, in bad taste. In 1838 the *North American Review* carried an especially bristly essay attacking American poets and novelists for falsely representing the Indians as picturesque and poetic. In reality, the essay contends, there is nothing "pleasing to the imagination in the dirty and smoky cabin of the Indian chief; there is nothing romantic in his custom of sleeping away the days . . . ; there is not a particle of chivalry in the contempt with which he regards his squaw. . . . " Because the Indians have "an inherent antipathy to the forms of civilized life," they are therefore, by extension, inherently antipathetic to the forms of civilized *literature.*[62]

In 1842 the *Democratic Review* carried an attack on George H. Colton, author of a long poem titled *Tecumseh,* accusing him not only of writing badly but of choosing a wildly inappropriate subject for serious, mature poetry:

> And it may be legitimate in the literature of college compositions to inflate and embellish up to the dignity of the heroic the barren and brutal barbarism of savage character and life, but Mr. Colton has made a mistake which we hope he will not repeat, in regarding it as a suitable theme for poetry to move the heart or satisfy the mind of the grown world of civilization.[63]

Colton's poem was also reviewed by Emerson, in the *Dial* of July 1842. Emerson's reaction was almost exactly the opposite of that of the writer for the *Democratic Review.* He found the poem a "pleasing summer-day story" produced by a "cultivated writer, with a skillful ear," but criticized the poet for his lack of originality—his overreliance on "old books," especially those of Walter Scott. For Emerson, the problem was not that Colton had tried too hard to turn his "savage" Indian subjects into dignified literary heroes but that he had erred in the other direction by trying too hard to include the kinds of details that would particularize his heroes and make them identifiably Indian:

> The most Indian thing about the Indian is surely not his moccasins, or his calumet, his wampum, or his stone hatchet, but traits of character and sagacity, skill or passion; which would be intelligible at Paris or at Pekin, and which Scipio or Sidney, Lord Clive or Colonel Crockett would be as likely to exhibit as Osceola and Black Hawk.[64]

Emerson's comments on the poem suggest that he was willing to admit the Indians into American literature, but only on the condition that the writer make them "intelligible" by making them representative (military) men, thereby obscuring as much of their specific ethnic and historical identity as possible.[65]

The *North American Review* published a long review of Simms's fiction and essays in 1846 that attacked Simms both for his obsession with fostering a national literature and for his belief that the Indians were an appropriate subject for American writers. The reviewer cautioned that the rush to produce a national literature was leading American writers into committing violations of universal standards of good taste, as a result of their naive assumption that the most promising indigenous subjects were the Indians and the life of the frontier. Writers like Simms needed to recognize that "there is much which no skill can make poetical, much which no light of imagination can clothe with the radiance of artistic beauty, much which cannot, by any possible magic of literary genius, be raised out of the region of squalid, grovelling, repulsive vice and barbarism." This "sadly unpoetic side of American life," the reviewer continued, cannot be treated in literature "without violating the laws of ideal beauty, under which all the works of imagination must necessarily arrange themselves." There was no reason, the writer concluded, why the American genius had to play the bumpkin before the world and plant himself in the wilderness, among savages, cutting himself off from the refinements of civilized life.[66]

The frontier novels of James Fenimore Cooper provided reviewers of all persuasions frequent opportunities to engage the question of the Indians' place in American literature. Although Cooper's powers of invention were generally granted to be great—he was often compared favorably to the revered Walter Scott—the point on which reviewers were most likely to disagree was the accuracy of Cooper's depiction of his Indian characters. In an 1828 review of the writings of the Moravian missionary John Heckwelder, Lewis Cass (soon to become Andrew Jackson's secretary of war) complained that Heckwelder's softhearted representations of the Indians—which Cass took to be dangerously irresponsible *mis*representations—were already having a deleterious effect on American literature. Cass's chief example was Cooper, whom he accused of having an effete easterner's naivete and credulity. Had Cooper spent any time actually traveling beyond the frontiers, Cass contended, he would know that his fictional Indians "have no living prototype in our forests. . . . They are the Indians of Mr. Heckwelder, and not the fierce and crafty warriors and hunters, that roam through our forests."[67] A reviewer for the *New-England Magazine* in 1835 was willing to grant that Cooper had only Simms and Catherine Sedgwick to compete with for first place among American novelists, but still insisted that since none of the three had the faintest idea how to portray realistic Indian characters, readers needed to be reminded that their work constituted only a "beautiful fiction."[68]

As a result of attacks like these, Cooper eventually began to call his works *romances* to defend himself against the charge that his writing was irrelevant or irresponsible because he was misrepresenting the Indians.[69] In the now-famous preface to *The Deerslayer*, he made public his defense in language that Simms may well have been paraphrasing in his own defense of Americanness in literature:

> It is the privilege of all writers of fiction, more particularly when their works aspire to the elevation of romances, to present the *beau-ideal* of their characters to the reader. That it is which constitutes poetry, and to suppose that the red man is to be represented only in the squalid misery or in the degraded moral state that certainly more or less belongs to his condition, is, we apprehend, taking a very narrow view of an author's privileges. Such criticism would have deprived the world of even Homer.

Cooper's attempt at self-justification did not fully succeed, in part because his critics were prepared to shift the grounds of their attack from the issue of the verisimilitude of his Indian characters to the issue of their very presence in works that asked to be taken seriously as literature (a question that, significantly, still haunts Cooper's reputation today).

In 1852, a few months after Cooper's death, Francis Parkman wrote a lengthy assessment of the novelist's career for the *North*

American Review. He praised Cooper for being an American original, making the obligatory comparisons with Walter Scott. But Parkman also found that Cooper had several serious failings, the most damaging of which was the superficiality and downright tiresomeness of his Indian characters. Echoing Lewis Cass, Parkman found Cooper guilty of encouraging a sentimental strain in the writers who came after him; he named Cooper and the English poet Thomas Campbell (author of "Gertrude of Wyoming") as the two writers most responsible for "the fathering of those aboriginal heroes, lovers, and sages, who have long formed a petty nuisance in our literature." Significantly, Parkman took the opportunity of this review to comment on the status, at midcentury, of the effort to produce an indigenous American literature. Cooper had promised much in his early career, he noted, but had ultimately failed to fulfill his promise; "the purpose, the energy, the passion of America have never found their adequate expression on the printed page." The only books that Parkman saw as successfully reflecting anything of the national character were those that dealt with Indians and frontiersmen (his examples were *Nick of the Woods, The Life of David Crockett,* and *The Big Bear of Arkansas*), but he also pointed out that these works and others like them could never fully recommend themselves to that portion of the American public "who make pretensions to taste and refinement." Parkman was not willing, in short, to allow that the Indians of Cooper or any of his contemporaries had a place in a literature that discriminating and cultivated readers could welcome, with any enthusiasm, as truly representative of mature American culture.[70]

In 1849 the *North American Review* published a long, magisterial essay by James Russell Lowell on the subject of a national literature. The essay does not specifically take up the issue of Indians in American writing; however, Lowell's comments are given in the context of his review of Longfellow's *Kavanagh*, a novel that caricatures the evangelical literary nationalists like Simms and Cornelius Mathews. Lowell argues that there is no such thing as a national literature, since all great writing is universal rather than local in its subjects and its appeal, and that the scramble to produce one in America has been self-defeating: "The feeling that it was absolutely necessary to our respectability that we should have a literature, has been a material injury to such as we have had. Our criticism has oscillated between the two extremes of depreciation and overpraise." Nationalism, Lowell concludes, "is only a less narrow form of provincialism, a sublimer sort of clownishness and ill-manners." Interestingly, when Lowell in this essay offers his list of the writers who might be models for the Americans, they are all English: Shakespeare, Milton, Wordsworth, Coleridge. Homer is not there; he had evidently become the property of the literary nationalists, those who wanted to reclaim and revise the American "savages" for the sake of the American epic.[71]

While the debates about the place of the Indians in American literature continued in the more "highbrow" literary journals of the eastern seaboard after midcentury, the place of the real Indians in the western states and territories was being decided, with less and less public debate, by federal troops. And as the Indians were forced further out of the path of American expansion, the complex issues associated with the "Indian question," at least as it had been defined in the first half of the century, also began to be dislodged from the public consciousness. One sign of this settling of public reaction can be seen in the increasingly sanitized presentation, in the popular journals, of issues that had been provoking serious debate for the previous thirty years.

In 1850 a new American journal was launched, *Harper's New Monthly Magazine*, with an editorial policy apparently intended to gain as wide a readership as possible by being as neutral as possible; the aim of the magazine, according to the announcement in the first issue, was to keep the American public up-to-date by providing reports of the most recent national and international news and by reprinting the best and most representative articles, on a wide range of subjects, from other American and British journals. By the beginning of 1851, the magazine was well established and confidently pursuing its policy of keeping the American public informed. A survey of the second volume (December 1850–May 1851) gives some indication of what the editors assumed their American readers wanted and needed to hear on the subject of the Indians.

In the January issue the national news coverage included a report that the secretary of war was requesting an increase in U.S. military forces because of hostile actions by the Indians on the borders of Texas and New Mexico. The secretary found the existing army units inadequate to deal with the Indians: "To extirpate them, he calls upon Congress to raise one or more regiments of mounted men" (264). The February issue contained the announcement of a new work of art, a statue by Mr. Stephenson of Charleston. "It is a statue of great merit both in conception and execution. It represents a North American Indian who has just received a mortal wound from an arrow . . ." (416). By April *Harper's* was reporting that the Indian hostilities had spread further west and become more alarming: the Indians "seem to have determined upon a war of extinction, which of course meets with prompt retaliation; and the ultimate issue can be no matter of uncertainty. . . . It is reported that all the Indians from Oregon to the Colorado have leagued together, and have sworn eternal hostility to the white race" (701).

The May 1851 issue announced the near-completion of another sculpture containing an Indian, Horatio Greenough's *The Pioneers* (also known as the *Rescue* group)—the sculpture that was to be placed at the eastern entrance to the U.S. Capitol building in 1853 and to remain there until 1958. The *Harper's* reporter praised the statue for being, like Stephenson's, "a sublime conception grandly executed," and this time he provided an interpretation of the work's significance:

> The action of the group symbolizes the one unvarying story of the contest between civilized and uncivilized man. The pioneer, standing almost erect, in the pride of conscious superiority, has dashed upon one knee the Indian, whose relaxed form, and cowering face upturned despairingly, express premonitions of the inevitable doom awaiting him, against which all his efforts would be unavailing. The heavy brow, compressed lip, and firm chin of the white man announce him one of a race born to conquer and rule, not so much by mere strength as by undaunted courage and indomitable will. (852)

The reviewer's description of the Greenough statue suggests not only why he could praise it so enthusiastically but also why this statue was chosen to adorn the Capitol of the United States. As symbol, the statue reduces the complex history of Indian-white relations in the country to a master narrative, representing the "one unvarying story" of the superior white man's triumph over the doomed Indian. And as a finished work of art, the statue reflects the successful sublimation of the figure of the uncivilized Indian, the figure that had once posed as serious a threat to the reputation of American art as to the reputation of American domestic policies. Some of the most influential of the literary critics had declared the Indian character of poetry and fiction—doomed though he might be—an embarrassment to refined taste and a drug on the literary market. The "relaxed" and unthreatening form of Greenough's sculpted Indian, however, is no more disturbing to the critic than he is to the sculpted pioneer. Cast in stone as a fixed symbol, and perpetually awaiting his inevitable death, Greenough's Indian is reassuring in his pathos, his muteness, and his immobility. He has become part of a sublime—and thoroughly civilized—representation of a version of the American story that can be sanctioned by artist, critic, and politician.

2 | *Writing and Silence: Melville*

WHEN HERMAN MELVILLE agreed in 1853 to let himself be nominated for the U.S. consulship in Honolulu, his father-in-law's friend H. W. Bishop wrote a letter in support of the nomination. After noting that Melville belonged to one of the "most distinguished democratic families of this state," Bishop added this disclaimer: "What his political views now are, I hardly know. His literary tastes and habits have withdrawn him from party controversies."[1] The idea implied by Bishop's statement—that Melville's writing was for him an escape from politics—was until fairly recently one of the dominant assumptions of Melville criticism. A 1951 history of American literature, for example, describes Melville as a kind of intellectual recluse whose "work was generally unaffected by the main currents of his time."[2] That view has been significantly revised by more recent reexaminations of Melville's career, such as Michael Paul Rogin's argument that Melville's deliberate rejection of the Jacksonian sympathies of his family was not a retreat from politics but in fact a direct and well-considered response to "the central historical and public issues of his time."[3] My concern in this chapter is to reunite at least some of Melville's "political views" with his "literary tastes and habits" by focusing on his interest, as a writer, in the evolution of the rhetoric of American nationalism, especially as it was shaped by the presence of the American Indians.

Perhaps more than any of his contemporaries, Melville was conscious of the extent to which the process of imaging the American nation required at least the pretense of public consensus. His fiction indicates that he saw the evolving public discourse of nationalism as allowing for only a single, univocal version of the American story, a version that was to provoke him to deeper and deeper skepticism through the course of his career. Melville was certainly not the only writer to find serious limitations and distortions in the discourse of the American "political romance" (to borrow Rogin's term) of the mid-nineteenth century. His reaction to this discourse can be distinguished from others, however, in part because of his continuing fascination with the gaps or silences in the American story—that is, his fascination with what the discourse could not contain or accommodate without completely undermining itself.

George Catlin, writing about the Indians of the western United States in 1841, had theorized that the mind of an Indian "is a beautiful blank on which anything can be written if the proper means be taken."[4] The expansionist politicians of the mid-nineteenth century frequently presented a similar image of the land on which the Indians lived as a vast empty space, waiting to be inscribed with the next chapter of the growing American story. As William Phelps of Minnesota put it in an 1859 speech in Congress, "It was not right that this fair continent should remain a wilderness. . . . Its rivers and its streams were not made to whisper their music to surrounding forests, but to be the busy scene of industry and life, and vocal with the music of the water-wheel."[5] What Melville came to find in that same space, however, was not the inviting silence of mindless men and trees but the very different silence of a population that was being deliberately muted. Melville knew that the lie of the "beautiful blank" had been perpetuated since 1492, when the sailors who arrived on a populated continent that was in fact "just as old, and perhaps older than Asia" returned home "swearing it was all water and moonshine there."[6] His own writing addresses the lie of emptiness both by acknowledging the silence and by attempting to incorporate it—*as silence*—into his revised version of the American story.

The plot that seems to have fascinated Melville most, the one he kept rewriting and revising, is an account of the confident white American's unsettling encounter with the silent other, the representative of a world that lies beyond the limits of the American's own discourse. In Melville's plot, the American must work to turn this other into "a beautiful blank" for the inscription of his particular discourse, if he is not to be completely undermined; when the other resists, then he must be removed, or exterminated, or both. In the responses of Melville's Americans, then, the other is given two familiar alternatives: to be civilized—through incorporation (or translation) into the American discourse—or to become extinct—through exclusion from it. The process of these fictional encounters follows one of the two patterns that have been characterized by Tzvetan Todorov as defining the entire history of relations between colonizers and the others who become the colonized. The colonizer, Todorov says, either perceives the other as a human being who is essentially identical with himself and can therefore be assimilated into the colonizer's culture, or he perceives the other as essentially different from, and therefore inferior to, himself. When the other is perceived as inferior, he quickly becomes expendable. "These two elementary figures of the experience of alterity are both grounded in egocentrism, in the identification of our own values with values in general, of our *I* with the universe—in the conviction that the world is one."[7] By accepting the centrality of this encounter with the other to all of American experience, and by refusing to attempt to speak for or through the other, Melville was at once acknowledging the absence of the other's voice from the American story and at the same time confirming that the silence of the other is a necessary part of the truth of the story. In allowing the enigmatic and problematic silence to remain exactly that, by not writing over it, he was doing the thing for which he asserted he most admired Shakespeare: "And if I magnify Shakespeare, it is not so much for what he did do, as for what he did not do, or refrained from doing."[8]

When William L. Stone's biography of the Mohawk chief Brant appeared in 1838, one reviewer was so pleased with it that he urged Stone to write another Indian biography, perhaps about the Wampanoag chief Philip, but this time using the "aboriginal" point of view.[9] This reviewer envisioned exactly the kind of life story that Melville seemed to become more and more convinced ought never to be written, and could never be truthfully written, since it could only contribute to furthering and valorizing the dangerous lie of univocality. Throughout his career, Melville was fascinated by the biographies that *cannot* be written and the stories that *cannot* be truthfully told—at least not by the white American. In his first novel, *Typee,* he had spoken parenthetically of the atrocities committed by Europeans in the South Sea islands as constituting such a story: "These things are seldom proclaimed at home; they happen at the very ends of the earth; they are done in a corner, and there are none to reveal them."[10] By the time he wrote *Moby-Dick,* Melville had removed the untellable story from its parenthetical position, and from its distantly exotic setting, and made it the center of his own story about Americans. Ishmael's narrative pursues the great sperm whale as insistently as Ahab's ship does, because Ishmael knows that "As yet . . . the sperm whale, scientific or poetic, lives not complete in any literature. Far above all hunted whales, his is an unwritten life."[11] The markings on the skin of the sperm whale remind Ishmael of Indian hieroglyphics, chiseled on rocks above the Mississippi River: "Like those mystic rocks, too, the marked whale remains undecipherable" (400). While Ahab pursues Moby-Dick in order to master him physically, Ishmael pursues him, retrospectively but with his own kind of obsessive energy, in order to civilize or assimilate him through the combination of his "scientific" and "poetic" language—to master him through his discourse. Moby-Dick eludes both efforts, but for Melville, the silent otherness of the whale is precisely what generates all that does get written or read—the ravings of Ahab as well as the musings of Ishmael. (Ahab, the obsessive whale-hater, can himself be seen as a prototype of the Indian-hater par excellence of *The Confidence Man,* the enigmatic man of whom, we are told, "there can be no biography.")[12]

In *Pierre*, the untellable story is Isabel's; Pierre recognizes that "it was the essential and unavoidable mystery of her history itself, which had invested Isabel with such wonderful enigmas to him."[13] Isabel's silence is initially enticing; however, once he chooses to accept the necessity of her continued silence—and all that it means— Pierre is not only "hurled from beneath his own ancestral roof" (185), and thus dispossessed of his American inheritance, but can no longer produce the genteel, respectable *writing* that once won him praise from the American critical establishment. In understanding Isabel's silence, that is, Pierre is himself silenced as a writer. Significantly, as Pierre struggles to write, he hears in his imagination "the leap of the Texan Camanche" (302), the embodiment of the truths that he cannot escape but also cannot write.

Melville's most explicit treatments of the white American's compulsion to supply a voice for the silent other, or simply to write over the silence of the other, appear in "Bartleby, the Scrivener" and "Benito Cereno." The narrator of "Bartleby" is compelled to write about his brief experience with the silent scrivener even though he must begin his account with the admission that "no materials exist for a full and satisfactory biography of this man. It is an irreparable loss to literature. Bartleby was one of those beings of whom nothing is ascertainable, except from the original sources, and in his case those are very small."[14] The narrator attempts to explain Bartleby and thus contain him within his own discourse, to make him part of "literature," but fails because the discourse he understands and needs to validate cannot accommodate the figure of Bartleby within any of its available structures of meaning. And since the narrator cannot tolerate the silences of the living Bartleby, he must be rid of him. In "Benito Cereno," the American Amasa Delano is not much troubled by the other, the black slave Babo, as long as Babo masquerades as a dutiful servant who talks exactly as the white master would want his faithful servant to talk. Babo's cheerful obsequiousness, his posture of physical and mental abasement to the superior white man, helps to confirm Delano in his own "humane satisfaction" with the orderliness of the world around him (52), even strengthening his confidence in the "ever-watchful Providence above" (97). The white man's discourse, that is, accommodates the black man's calculated lies about himself very easily. When the masquerade ends, however, and the truth is revealed—that the black man's posing has been part of a complex scheme of vengeance against the white masters—Delano becomes violent and Babo, significantly, becomes silent; he does not speak from the time he is unmasked until he meets his "voiceless end" (116) on the gallows. The *real* Babo, of course, is silent in this text from the very beginning, since that is all he can be in the white American's story, whether it is told by Delano or by Melville.

This repeated acknowledging of the lives that cannot be represented in American writing is consistent with Melville's general distrust of all thinking that does not allow for mystery, ambiguity, and uncertainty. As Ishmael puts it in *Moby-Dick*, "Whatever is truly wondrous and fearful in man, never yet was put into words or books" (607). Yet his attitude also suggests a more specific distrust of much that was being said by his contemporaries about the place of the Indians in American writing. Many of the nineteenth-century writers who portrayed Indians—whether they took the "scientific" or the "poetic" approach, to use Ishmael's categories—included in their texts some justification for taking up the subject in the first place. The obvious justification, and the one most frequently used, was that the Indians themselves did not write, and since virtually everyone agreed that the Indians were likely to become extinct very soon, many white writers expressed a sense of urgency about "catching" the Indians before they disappeared. William L. Stone prefaced his biography of Brant with a typical description of the Indians as "that brave and ill-used race of men, now melting away before the Anglo-Saxons like the snow beneath a vertical sun. . . . No Indian pen traces the history of their tribes and nations, or records the deeds of their warriors and chiefs—their prowess and their wrongs."[15]

Stone's point was reiterated by George Catlin in the opening of his *Letters and Notes on the Manners, Customs, and Conditions of the North American Indians*. Catlin described himself as "lending a hand to a dying nation, who have no historians or biographers of their own to pourtray [*sic*] with fidelity their native looks and history" (1:3). Both Stone and Catlin thus offer themselves as sympathetic chroniclers who can provide white audiences with accurate, faithful accounts of Indian lives. Washington Irving, on the other hand, after giving a very brief sketch of the "Traits of Indian Character," admits that he sees nothing more to be done except to consign the rest of the story to the white mythologizers, to do with as they will: "[The Indians] will vanish like a vapour from the face of the earth; their very history will be lost in forgetfulness. . . . Or if, perchance, some dubious memorial of them should survive, it may be in the romantic dreams of the poet, to people in imagination his glades and groves, like the fauns and satyrs and sylvan deities of antiquity."[16]

Melville, who distrusted "confidence men" and yea-sayers in general, was especially distrustful of this effort to supply a history or biography, even a mythic history, for those people whose real lives had remained inaccessible to white Americans, for whatever reason. He was preoccupied with the presence of those unarticulated lives from the beginning of his career, but his attitude toward them and toward the writers who attempted to articulate them, and therby situate them within a common discourse, became increasingly more complex and more inextricable from his attitude toward the larger project of chronicling American history. One important indication of this change can be seen in his shifting responses to some of those other writers who had set out to explain the Indians to a white American audience.

In his first novel, *Typee* (1846), Melville was already addressing the relevance of the distinction between savagery and civilization, a distinction that still figured prominently in American theorizing about the "Indian question." In asking rhetorically, "How often is the term 'savage' incorrectly applied" (27), Melville echoes George Catlin's earlier observation that "the very use of the word savage, as it is applied in its general sense, I am inclined to believe is an abuse of the word, and the people to whom it is applied" (1:9). In fact, the sojourn of Melville's narrator, Tommo, among the Marquesans leads him to many of the same conclusions that Catlin reaches after traveling among the North American Indians. Whether Melville had read Catlin or not when he wrote *Typee* (and it seems to me likely that he had), they are in general agreement about Anglo-European misconceptions of the "savage" other. However, while both see the civilization/savagery dichotomy as false and unjust, both still repeat some of the hoariest clichés to which that distinction had given rise. Melville's islanders and Catlin's Indians are all presented as happy innocents, not yet contaminated by the vices of civilization. Melville's Fayaway, for example, is a "child of nature" who enjoys "a perfect freedom from care and anxiety" (86). In their isolation, she and her "unsophisticated" people (15) are far happier than the "self-complacent European" (124). Similarly, Catlin finds his Indians "in their primitive state, as the Great Spirit made and endowed them with good hearts and kind feelings, unalloyed and untainted by the views of the money-making world" (1:61). Tommo and Catlin, in short, return from their two journeys among primitive people full of similar news about a remarkable discovery: the noble savage.

Both Catlin and Melville also repeat a cliché that was often heard during the debates on Indian removal in the 1830s: the idea that uncivilized people are immediately contaminated and degraded by contact with white civilization. When Melville's "poor savages" are put in the company of white sailors, "they are easily led into every vice, and humanity weeps over the ruin thus remorselessly inflicted upon them by their European civilizers" (15). Melville's shipboard world is the floating equivalent of Catlin's American frontier, which Catlin calls the place of "savage degradation; where the genius of natural liberty and independence have been blasted and destroyed by the contaminating vices and dissipations introduced by the immoral part of *civilized* society" (1:60). Like Catlin, Melville is clearly sympathetic with his primitives and incensed at the treatment they have frequently received from European intruders, but his account of the Marquesans only reinforces the idea that the otherness of the islanders, like that of Catlin's Indians, necessarily makes them inferior to the Anglo-Europeans (including Melville and Catlin); they are victimized because they are so simple as to be incapable of understanding the duplicitous motives of the more complex whites. Both writers, that is, attempt only to shift the weight of the *moral* values attached to the definitions of civilization and savagery at the same time that they naively accept the definitions themselves. Furthermore, Melville's Tommo obviously thinks of himself as a captive among the Marquesans; he never fully trusts them, and he risks death to escape them and make his way back to the "feverish civilization" (125) he so fully condemns. Back in civilized America, the sailor-turned-writer produces the same kind of melancholy epitaph for the Marquesans that Catlin, Stone, Irving, and others had produced for the North American Indians: "Ill-fated people! I shudder when I think of the change a few years will produce in their paradisaical abode" (195).

Through Tommo, then, Melville was only adding his voice (rather belatedly) to those that had already established one formulaic pattern for the white American's response to his encounter with the other: Melville denounces the white supremacist's view of the savage at the same time that he reinforces that view by presenting his islanders as childlike, limited, and doomed to disappear before the progress of the cannier whites. Melville was to create another version of Tommo later in Captain Delano of "Benito Cereno," a character whose impulses are every bit as genial and philanthropic as Tommo's (and Catlin's). Just as Tommo finds the Marquesan women who come on board his ship "unsophisticated and confiding" (15), for example, Delano finds the African women on the slave ship "unsophisticated as leopardesses; loving as doves" (73). But the crucial difference between these two versions of the humane white American is that the second version is thoroughly and egregiously ironic; Delano's self-consciously generous impulses lead him to misread completely the signs around him—to forget, for one thing, that leopardesses can also be wily and extremely dangerous when threatened. By the time of "Benito Cereno," then, Melville had moved far beyond his own early effort to interpret the savage other; the later text helps to define the earlier one as an exercise in psychological projection, a willful turning of the other into a blank space for the inscription of the writer/interpreter's own discourse. Significantly, however, Melville had also by this time come to see the effort at inscription as central to every previous telling of the American story, including his own, and as essential to the whole public project of American self-definition.

In *Moby-Dick*, Melville returns to the distinction between civilized and savage, this time deliberately blurring it by reminding the reader often that his American whalemen, whose job it is to slaughter as many whales as possible, are the contemporary equivalents of the savage hunters they have replaced. The *Pequod* sails from Nantucket, and "where else but from Nantucket did those aboriginal whalemen, the Red-Men, first sally out in canoes to give chase to the Leviathan?" (31). In Melville's covert scheme in the novel, commercial, expansionist America has taken on the characteristics of the people who had earlier been methodically dispossessed because they were, in white America's terms, too thoroughly savage to be part of civilized America. Now, Ahab on his "cannibal of a craft" (105) pursues the "devilish" (692) whale through a bloodied ocean—and all this with the full blessing of the Quaker owners, whose chief concern is to turn a good profit. The treatment of the concept of savagery is far more complex and convincing in this book than it is in *Typee* because this time Melville sets out not just to play with the simple formulas that produce the naive civilization/savagery dichotomy but to explode them.

The character in *Moby-Dick* who clings most blithely to the old formulas is Ishmael, the one who records the story. Because he is the would-be biographer of both Ahab and Moby-Dick, Ishmael wants to believe that his sojourn on the sea, among wild men, has qualified him to write about his two subjects by making him more like them. He indulges in the fantasy that in the course of the whaling voyage he has undergone a full-scale reversion to savagery: "Long exile from Christendom and civilization inevitably restores a man to that condition in which God placed him, i.e. what is called savagery. Your true whale-hunter is as much a savage as an Iroquois. I myself am a savage . . . " (358). Ishmael's serene, *written* pronouncement about himself, which relies on an Anglo-European, Christian conception of savagery, especially on its association of nomadic hunting with the savage state, is ironically self-canceling.

(Would a mid-nineteenth-century Iroquois call himself, in writing, a savage?) What the statement really tells us is that Ishmael would *like* to feel far removed from the self that he is on the land; he would *like*, at the same time, to believe that his language has not been deracinated, that his experience has made him capable of writing an intelligible, convincing book about savage subjects.

On the other hand, the character whose behavior we might most appropriately describe as savage is Ahab, and the source of his savage obsession is not, as Ishmael would have it, in his removal from "Christendom and civilization" but, rather, in his frustrated effort to live an unconflicted life as a Christian and a civilized man. As Ishmael notes, "Though nominally included in the census of Christendom, he was still an alien to it" (206). Ahab deliberately goes to sea in order to do final battle with the instincts and desires in himself that *he* sees as savage. For him, the hunting of the whale is an attempt to externalize those impulses that he thinks estrange him spiritually and psychologically from the culture of white Christian America, to confront them and destroy them, or be destroyed himself. Ahab may see himself as the antitype of the good Christian and the good American, but Melville knows that he is in fact one type of the American self, so pure a type as to seem a kind of grotesque anachronism; he believes as deeply as any New England Puritan divine ever did that the opaque other, the savage, is demonic and must be exterminated, that the savage and the civilized man cannot inhabit the same space for long—especially not the same self.

When the Quaker owners of the *Pequod*, Captains Peleg and Bildad, send the ship off, their parting advice to the sailors is to remember their prayers, to keep the Sabbath, to beware of fornication, and to make as much money as they can. They are comfortable with their gentrified, watered-down versions of the Christian and the capitalist imperatives because, apparently, the two imperatives remain separate for them. Ishmael, for example, wonders how Peleg can reconcile his piety with the spilling of "tuns upon tuns of leviathan gore," and concludes that it must be because "he had long since come to the sage and sensible conclusion that a man's religion is one thing, and this practical world quite another" (112). For Ahab, on the other hand, religion and the business of the world are anything but separate. For him, this whaling voyage is no less than a crusade against the Leviathan, and the spiritual consequences are as immediate and real for him as they were for his great cultural progenitor, the man Melville calls in another place "doleful, ghostly, ghastly Cotton Mather."[17] Peleg and Bildad kill whales to make money, but Mather and Ahab set out to kill the Leviathan in order to save themselves and preserve all of "Christendom and civilization." Mather recorded with approval the beginning of the process by which the Indian, his Leviathan, was removed from the civilization of white America. By resurrecting his particular obsessions in Ahab, Melville reminds us, first, that Mather's is an archetypal American story, and second, that what Mather did not include in his account is the acknowledgement that the real demons he was pursuing were within. As Richard Slotkin has said,

> Mather entered the wilderness of the human mind bent on extirpating its 'Indians,' exorcizing its demons. These Indian-demons were the impulses of the unconscious—the sexual impulses, the obscure longings and hatreds that mark parent-child relationships, the proddings of a deep-rooted sense of guilt. The goal of his therapy was to eliminate these impulses, to cleanse the mind of them utterly, to purge it and leave it pure.[18]

The Mather whom Slotkin describes here is the "ghastly" one who fascinated (and disturbed) Melville, the one in whose compulsive hatred of the demonic Leviathan we can recognize the ultimate origins of Ahab's own obsessive need to project and then to exorcize.

The linking of Ahab and Mather through a common cultural genealogy is reinforced by Melville's many references to the colonial histories (including Mather's) of the early encounters between the New England Puritans and the Indians. Ishmael tells us that the name of Ahab's ship, the *Pequod*, "was the name of a celebrated tribe of Massachusetts Indians, now extinct as the ancient Medes" (104). What he does not say explicitly is that the tribe became extinct because they were deliberately exterminated by the white colonists. In his account of the Pequod (or Pequot, as Mather spells it) War in the

Magnalia Christi Americana, Mather reports that the first Puritan settlers found that "these parts were then covered with nations of babarous Indians and infidels, in whom the 'prince of the power of the air' did 'work in a spirit.' " Of these Indians, Mather continues, "there was none more fierce, more warlike, more potent, or of a greater terror unto their neighbors, than that of the Pequods." The response of the colonists to the perceived ferocity of the Pequods was to massacre them; Mather recounts with satisfaction the burning of a Pequod fort—containing men, women, and children—in May of 1637: "In a little more than one hour, five or six hundred of these barbarians were dismissed from a world that was burdened with them."[19] Another early chronicler of the Pequod War, Edward Johnson, concurred with Mather's interpretation of the decimating of the Pequods: "Thus by their horrible pride," Johnson wrote, "they fitted themselves for destruction."[20]

In setting his story on board a ship called the *Pequod*, whose captain has committed himself (and the lives of all those who have chosen to join him) to the destruction of the Leviathan, Melville therefore calls up one of the oldest indigenous versions of the New England story. The structure of the old story and many of its crucial tropes and symbols are still appropriate; they work as well to describe a nineteenth-century voyage out of Massachusetts as they did to describe a seventeenth-century venture into it. We can see the way Melville deliberately plunders the old narratives to find details for his story by considering, as one example, the number and kind of his allusions to the colonial accounts of King Philip's War (1675–1676). When Philip (as the colonists rechristened him; his original Wampanoag name is variously given as Metacom, Metacomet, or Pometacom) was finally hunted down and killed by the colonial militia, his head was cut off and sent to Plymouth, where the church happened to be holding a thanksgiving service. Mather found the occasion particularly significant: "God sent 'em in the head of a Leviathan for a *thanksgiving feast*" (2:576). Philip's head remained, for twenty years, displayed on a gibbet in Plymouth, where Mather evidently found it: "It was not long before this hand which now writes, upon a certain occasion took off the jaw from the exposed skull of that Blasphemous Leviathan; and the renowned Samuel Lee hath since been a pastor to an English congregation, sounding and showing the praises of Heaven, upon that very spot of ground where *Philip* and his Indians were lately worshipping of the Devil.'"[21]

On the deck of Melville's *Pequod*, Ishmael also finds the remains of the Leviathan's skull, in the form of "a strange sort of tent, or rather wigwam," that has been made from "the jaws of the right-whale"; at the point of this wigwam, "the loose hairy fibres waved to and fro like the top-knot on some old Pottowottamie sachem's head" (106). From within this structure, Peleg and Bildad issue forth to conduct their business: recruiting sailors to kill whales and giving out religious tracts. One of the men they recruit is the "savage" Queequeg, the scion of a royal cannibal family, whose name Melville probably took from that of another son of royalty, the Narragansett Indian Queequegunent. While Queequegunent is not mentioned in Mather's *Magnalia*, he does appear in Samuel Drake's account of King Philip's War in his *Biography and History of the Indians of North America*. Drake notes that Queequegunent was the son of a squaw-sachem named Magnus, who was herself the sister of one sachem and the daughter-in-law of another. Magnus was killed by the British during King Philip's War, but almost all that is known of her son is that he signed a treaty in 1660 (signing, as Queequeg signs the ship's papers, with "his mark") that mortagaged all of the Narragansett country to the state of Connecticut.[22]

Melville may also have been drawing on yet another account of King Philip's War, Benjamin Church's *Entertaining Passages Relating to Philip's War*. Church's narrative was first published in 1716 and had been reprinted at least seventeen times by 1850. It was Church who finally succeeded in tracking down and killing Philip, at the head of a small army made up of white colonists and "friend-Indians" recruited by Church. Like Ahab, Church was wounded in the leg in an early encounter with Philip's Indians; he returned home to his wife and child for a while, again like Ahab, but was soon persuaded to join another expedition against Philip. Church's army was as heterogeneous as Ahab's crew, and he seemed to have the same charismatic effect on the Indians he recruited for his army as

Ahab has on his sailor-savages: "For there was none of them but, after they had been a little while with him," Church wrote, referring to himself in the third person, "would be as ready to pilot him to any place where the Indians dwelt or haunted (though their own fathers or nearest relations should be among them), or fight for him, as any of his own men."[23]

Ishmael's breezy comment about the "Red-Men" who sallied out of Nantucket "to give chase to the Leviathan" therefore introduces a complicated network of related allusions by which Melville anchors his story in one of the oldest versions of the American story. In both versions, the American hero, the man of faith and energy—Ishmael's "man of greatly superior natural force" (111)—becomes savagely bloodthirsty through the very intensity of his hatred of the opaque savage other. And Melville clearly suggests that the psychic energy that drives a Mather or an Ahab to create the Leviathan by naming it, then to seek it out and exterminate it, still works in the America of 1851 to drive white expansion westward.[24]

In his 1849 review of Francis Parkman's *Oregon Trail*, Melville had noted the similarity between frontier adventurers and sea adventurers: when western travelers "cast off their horses' halters from the post before the log-cabin door, they do as sailors, when they unmoor their cables, and set sail for sea."[25] As the *Pequod* nears its encounter with Moby-Dick, Ishmael describes the ship as crossing "these sea-pastures, wide-rolling watery prairies" (613). At times it seems as if the *Pequod* is "struggling forward, not through high rolling waves, but through the tall grass of a rolling prairie: as when the western emigrants' horses only show their erected ears, while their hidden bodies widely wade through the amazing verdure" (623). The white emigration across the prairies in the 1840s toward the land and the gold of the West Coast intensified white America's violent conflict with the Indian, the old Leviathan, and necessitated a renewal of the rhetoric that would justify what was, in actuality, the white culture's savage project of extermination. As *Harper's* magazine reported in early 1851, the influx of emigrants into California had resulted in "desperate hostilities between the Indians and the whites. The former seem to have determined upon a war of extermination . . . and the ultimate issue can be no matter of uncertainty."[26] The civilized person and the savage, the Christian and the Leviathan, still cannot inhabit the same continent in the mid-nineteenth-century rewriting of the *Magnalia*.

In this context, it is especially interesting that Melville's narrator, his chronicler, is the mild, commonsensical, and noncommital Ishmael, for whom the metaphysical and/or theological implications of the whale hunt are at best curious and at worst embarrassing. From Ishmael's perspective, *both* Queequeg's "savage" religion and the "civilized" doctrines of Christianity are merely forms of superstition. Although he is clearly fascinated by the possibilities of interpretation offered by the several theologies available to him, he ultimately rejects them all in favor of a more placidly pragmatic stance. He tries to talk Queequeg out of his idol worship, for example, but only because he finds it foolish and contrary to "the laws of Hygiene and common sense" (125). Watching the Indian Tashtego, on the other hand, he thinks (echoing Mather) that "you would almost have credited the superstitions of some of the earlier Puritans, and half believed this wild Indian to be a son of the Prince of the Air" (165). Ishmael insulates himself, emotionally and psychologically, willfully holding to his intention of experiencing the voyage only as a means of therapeutic purgation, a way of "driving off the spleen, and regulating the circulation"; it is precisely because of his ability to dodge significances, to avoid "growing grim about the mouth" (23), that he is willing and able to take on the role of historian of the voyage.

Ishmael survives to tell his version of the story, that is, because he does not really comprehend or participate in Ahab's version of it. He is, as Gary Lindberg has said of him, a shape-shifter and jack-of-all-trades who "preserves his general sanity and his freedom from obsession by successively disengaging himself from each role, by knowing how to work from the center outwards into many alternative possibilities."[27] This analysis of Ishmael's physical and psychological salvation, however, does not take sufficient account of the implications of his role as a privileged chronicler, the only narrator of a story about the darkly obsessive "center" of American history and culture. Ishmael frees himself from obsession only by freeing himself from history and memory, taking refuge in the inevitably spurious language and structure of his own "free" discourse. He is Melville's version of the new American chronicler, who cannot, or will not, understand the chief actors—Ahab, Queequeg, Moby Dick—in the story he tells. If he did fully understand the implications of his story, and if he did take it literally, he would no more attempt to preserve the story in writing than Ahab would. He, too, would be at best silenced by it, and at worst destroyed.

In "Bartleby, the Scrivener" Melville created another narrator who, more obviously than Ishmael, is able to tell his story precisely because his recourse to the institutions of "civilization," including its forms of discourse, saves him from a full understanding of the matter of his story. This narrator acknowledges right away that he cannot tell the whole story of Bartleby, since "no materials exist for a full and satisfactory biography of this man" (13). What he tells instead is the story of his effort to understand and thus to save Bartleby—the enigmatic other—by bringing him within the range of his own discourse. His effort fails; the living Bartleby cannot be accommodated in the narrator's Wall Street office, nor in his narrative, whether we take the narrative to be primarily biographical or autobiographical. In effect, the narrator offers Bartleby two choices: to become "civilized" through assimilation or to become extinct. When Bartleby resists assimilation, he is removed and left to die, without having told his story; the narrator remains to write his own version of the encounter with Bartleby, to lament Bartleby's death, and to declare that the absence of a full and complete biography of Bartleby is "an irreparable loss to literature" (13). What remains is a removal story, told by the remover.

Although this narrator is like Ishmael in shielding himself from a full understanding of his own story, he differs from Ishmael in two very important ways. First, this narrator makes his living by writing, even though the writing is confined to the drawing up and copying of legal documents. And second, he is a willing participant in the most mundane and least adventurous aspects of the life of commercial America, a lawyer who covets soft patronage appointments and loves money. Melville makes it clear that he finds those two characteristics of his narrator perfectly congenial and consistent with each other; in the Wall Street world of this story, the amount of writing one is rewarded for is directly proportional to the amount of self one is willing to yield up to the common commercial enterprise. The one great, troubling hiatus in the narrator's otherwise prudent and well-rewarded career is the brief appearance of Bartleby, who refuses to contribute to that common enterprise by copying documents and who cannot himself be "copied" into the narrator's account.

If we see the narrator as deliberately attempting to rid himself of the haunting, guilt-inducing specter of Bartleby in writing this self-justifying narrative, then we can begin to understand why in introducing himself he refers three times to a man with whom he has apparently had only incidental contact, John Jacob Astor. The narrator chooses Astor as his patron, the true recipient of his narrative, as if by merely invoking the talismanic name he might be absolved from whatever guilt and self-recrimination he has incurred from his encounter with Bartleby. The reiteration of Astor's name at the beginning of the story also suggests that Melville may well have been responding to two other contemporary narratives that also begin with deference to Astor, the memoirs of the Washington lawyer Thomas L. McKenney and the *Astoria* of the successful writer Washington Irving.

Thomas McKenney directed the Office of Indian Trade from 1816 to 1822; in 1824 he was appointed first director of the newly created Bureau of Indian Affairs, where he remained until he was removed from office by Andrew Jackson in 1830. In the first position his major accomplishment was to design and push through Congress the Indian Civilization Act (1819), the primary purpose of which was to establish a system of schools to teach Indian children English and agriculture. As director of the Bureau of Indian Affairs, he became the chief architect of the important Indian Removal Act (1830), which provided the legal authority for removing eastern tribes to territory west of the Mississippi. The general shape of McKenney's career as a manager of Indian affairs, therefore, closely resembles the shape of the narrator's relationship to Bartleby: both first attempted to civilize or assimilate their charges, and then both resorted to removing them.

There are, however, more specific and compelling reasons for finding in McKenney one model for Melville's narrator. Like the narrator, McKenney was removed from office by a change in administration; McKenney lost his post in the Bureau of Indian Affairs, and the narrator lost his mastership in chancery. McKenney's resentment at his firing (by Andrew Jackson) and his wish to redeem his self-image—again like the narrator's—seem to have had a great deal to do with his writing about himself in the first place. McKenney also begins his *Memoirs, Official and Personal* (published in 1846) with a bow to John Jacob Astor, whom McKenney calls "a sagacious and wonderful man,"[28] as if the very mention of the name of Astor were enough to establish McKenney's own credentials and remove some of the tarnish from his public reputation. He then goes on to defend himself and his reputation by contrasting his own humanitarianism (in the treatment of both his employees and the Indians under his charge) with the arbitrary and inhumane treatment he received from his superiors. McKenney goes out of his way to acknowledge the assistance of his clerks in the Bureau of Indian Affairs, and to explain the nature of his relationship with them:

> No one who has not experienced it can know how strong the ties become between the head of a department and his clerks, provided there is mutual zeal, and a corresponding intelligence, to carry on the business entrusted to each, in his sphere. . . . To dismiss from office, in those days, without cause—and there could be no cause for turning an incumbent out of office except *incompetency, neglect of duty,* or *dishonesty* . . . would have been deemed an outrage, no less against the public interests, than the party proscribed. . . . [I]t no more occurred to me to turn them out, than it did to cut their throats. (1:24)

In defending himself as an employer of clerks, McKenney is also clearly attacking the employer who, he implies, cut McKenney's own throat by removing him without just cause. We can see precisely the same psychological pattern working in Melville's narrator, who takes great pains to let us know that as irritating as his clerks Turkey and Nippers can be, he is too humane a man to treat them as he himself was treated and remove them from their jobs.

Interestingly, one of the clerks that McKenney hired for the bureau was a young Choctaw Indian, James Lawrence McDonald, who had been educated in a Quaker school for Indians financed by the War Department. In 1818, when McDonald was in his teens, he was sent to Washington as a kind of showcase example of the value of educating Indians at the hands of white Christians. He was soon passed on to McKenney, who took him into his home and gave him a job as clerk in his office. McDonald's chief job was, like Bartleby's, to copy the letters of his patron. In his published memoirs, McKenney tells the story of the failure of his scheme to make McDonald into the first successful Indian lawyer. When he first proposed a legal career to his ward, McDonald was, according to McKenney's reconstruction of their conversation, grateful but reluctant: " 'Ah, sir, being an Indian, I am marked with a mark as deep and abiding as that which Cain bore. My race is degraded—trodden upon—despised' " (2:113). When McKenney persisted, McDonald agreed to study law, but instead of returning to work with McKenney after his training he went back to his tribe and, again according to McKenney, took to drinking hard. The two men met once more when McDonald appeared in Washington as the legal representative of a delegation of Choctaws. McKenney's version of his treatment of McDonald on that occasion could just as easily have come from Melville's narrator: "I sought all proper opportunities to restore him. On one occasion I detained him in my office, after the rest of the delegation had retired, and locking the door, spoke to him on his fall with every tenderness that I could employ" (2:116). McDonald, however, like Bartleby, rejected the paternal advice of his employer and left Washington with the other Choctaws. He died not long after, in a fall that McKenney interpreted as an act of suicide.[29]

McKenney also attempts in his *Memoirs* to clear his name by presenting himself as a man whose interest in the Indians was entirely benign and humanitarian. He is especially concerned to make it clear that although he urged the voluntary removal of the eastern

Indians for their own good, he was surprised and appalled by the forced removals that followed passage of the 1830 Removal Act. Even though he found the state of the Indians "painful," he protested that he was always convinced that "the Indian was, in his intellectual and moral structure, *our equal*" (1:34). It was up to benevolent and paternal whites, McKenney argued, to save the Indians from the extinction that seemed imminent: "The cry from the forests, from the beginning, and that which is heard to this hour, and which has never been hushed for over two hundred years, is, ' PROTECT US— PROTECT US—PITY AND SAVE US!' " (1:93). After a few years of trying to save the Indians by civilizing them where they were, McKenney shifted his ground and urged that they could be saved from extinction only by removing them to a place of isolation and safety.

Again the parallels with Melville's narrator seem clear. The narrator wants to save Bartleby because he finds his presence painful: he is "touched and disconcerted" (21) by the strangeness of this clerk who prefers not to contribute to the business of the office and whose behavior does not fit any pattern that he can recognize. Furthermore, in his baffled attempt to come to some determination about what to do with Bartleby and his eventual decision that Bartleby must be gotten out of the way, the narrator goes through a psychological process that reproduces, in small, the process by which McKenney and others in positions of authority decided that the Indians must be removed from all those places where the business of America was being successfully transacted. For the narrator, this process takes him from believing that he can "cheaply purchase a delicious self-approval" (23) by offering Bartleby his paternalistic tolerance to attempting eventually to regain some small portion of his *lost* self-approval by explaining in his narrative that even if his efforts to save Bartleby failed, his humanitarian intentions never did.

At first, the narrator attempts to divert his anger at the resisting Bartleby into the same kind of vaguely Christian, assimilationist attitude that McKenney had taken. "A fraternal melancholy!" the narrator says; "For both I and Bartleby were sons of Adam" (28). The narrator's smug comment ironizes the fuzzy humanitarianism of both his position and McKenney's, since, for one thing, we know that one of the sons of Adam destroyed the other and bore the mark of his guilt for the rest of his life. But Melville may also have been reflecting ironically on some of his own earlier published statements, such as those he had made in *Typee* or, more recently, in his 1849 review of Parkman's *Oregon Trail*. Melville had criticized Parkman for the "disdain and contempt" he had shown toward the Indians, arguing that Parkman's superior attitude was not only wrong but indefensible: "We are all of us—Anglo-Saxons, Dyaks, and Indians—sprung from one head and made in one image. And if we reject this brotherhood now, we shall be forced to join hands hereafter."[30] Melville may, that is, have been acknowledging through a moment of oblique self-parody in "Bartleby" that even his own publicly expressed humanitarianism masked deeper, more complex, and guiltier feelings toward the Indians than he had heretofore been willing to acknowledge.

When the "haughtiness" and "reserve" (28) of Bartleby finally drive the narrator to determine that the offending scrivener can no longer remain in the office, he resorts to a series of justifications for his decision that are again strongly reminiscent of the arguments that had been made to justify the removal of the Indians. He finds Bartleby ungrateful and unresponsive, "considering the undeniable good usage and indulgence he had received" (30); he notes that Bartleby pays no rent and no taxes, and does not own the place he inhabits (95), yet he fears that Bartleby might "outlive me, and claim possession of my office by his perpetual occupancy" (38). Most significantly, he offers to help Bartleby with his money and his influence, as McKenney and Andrew Jackson had offered to help the Cherokees, "if he himself would take the first step towards a removal" (32).

When Bartleby still refuses to go, the narrator reacts in exactly the way McKenney had reacted to the refusal of the Cherokees to remove themselves voluntarily from the land they had claimed as theirs by their own insistence on the right of "perpetual occupancy"; he turns his back, unwilling to participate in a *forced* removal and pitying the one removed, yet finally acquiesing in a process that his own acts had, in fact, set in motion: "The landlord's energetic, summary disposition," the narrator says, "had led him to adopt a procedure which I do not think I would have decided upon myself; and yet as a last resort, under such peculiar circumstances, it seemed the only plan" (42). As a result of the landlord's ultimatum, Bartleby is taken away on his own private Trail of Tears; he is conducted in "a silent procession" (42) across what the narrator has already referred to, significantly, as "the Mississippi of Broadway" (28) and led to the place where he will be confined, and where he will (as many of the transported Cherokees did) starve to death.[31]

The other possible source for "Bartleby" that I want to examine, Washington Irving's *Astoria* (1836), is also a book that is to some extent about the problem of what white America was to do about the Indians, whose lives Irving describes as "little better than a prolonged and all-besetting death."[32] The most immediate purpose of Irving's book, however, is to celebrate the career of John Jacob Astor, one of those men "who by their great commercial enterprises have enriched nations, peopled wildernesses, and extended the bounds of empire" (39). Astor's name and character, Irving says, "are worthy of being enrolled in the history of commerce" (27), while of the Indians, he predicts, "in a little while scarcely any traces will be left" (223). History, that is, will remember and honor men like Astor, whose pioneering ventures in "the keen activity of private enterprise" (27) draw the culture of commercial America westward, while the Indians, for whom the white culture's veneration of capitalistic enterprise is nearly inexplicable, will understandably fade from the collective American memory. The entire history of these uncivilized people, Irving says, "is an enigma, and a grand one—will it ever be solved?" (227). In writing his own history of Astor's successes, therefore, Irving helps to guarantee that his prediction—about whose lives will be inscribed in American history and whose will not—will come true.

Melville was given a set of Irving's works in June of 1853,[33] and we know that he probably wrote the whole of "Bartleby" during the latter part of that same summer; it is at least reasonable to assume, then, that he had Irving on his mind when he wrote the story. His attitude toward the immensely popular Irving seems to have been ambivalent at best. In "Hawthorne and His Mosses" (1850), for example, Melville had praised the complexity and difficulty of Haw-

thorne's work, contrasting it with the work of a writer whom he does
not name but who sounds very much like Irving:

> But that graceful writer, who perhaps of all Americans has received
> the most plaudits from his own country for his productions,—that
> very popular and amiable writer, however good, and self-reliant in
> many things, perhaps owes his chief reputation to the self-
> acknowledged imitation of a foreign model, and to the studied avoid-
> ance of all topics but smooth ones. (247)

What Melville clearly implies here (as he also does in *Pierre*) is that
in America, the writer is rewarded for imitation (Irving acknowledged
that his model and mentor was Walter Scott) and for the graceful
treatment of safe or "smooth" topics. That same formula for success
is the one that the narrator of "Bartleby," who is "a drawer-up of
recondite documents" (19), claims rather smugly to be his own. He
calls himself an "eminently safe man," one who has always believed
"that the easiest way of life is the best" (14). It was his very lack of
ambition and energy, he says, that first recommended him to Astor,
a man by whom he was employed (as was Irving) to write.

If Irving himself suggests a model for the narrator, his *Astoria*
also contains likely models for the two eccentric clerks in "Bartleby,"
Turkey and Nippers.[34] Irving describes in some detail the voyage of
the ship that Astor sent to his isolated trading station on the Columbia River and the problems caused for the ship's captain by two of
Astor's employees, Stuart and McDougal. Stuart he describes as "an
easy soul, and of a social disposition" (57), while McDougal is "an
active, irritable, fuming, vainglorious little man" (54). The two thus
resemble Turkey and Nippers in their morning moods, when Turkey
is "the blandest and most reverential of men" (15), while Nippers
reveals his "testiness and grinning irritability" (16). Turkey and Nippers create the same difficulty for their employer as Stuart and
McDougal do for the ship captain, who was, Irving says, first "crossed
by the irritable mood of one" and then "excessively annoyed by the
good-humor of another" (57).

Both Irving and Melville's narrator linger over their descriptions
of the eccentric employees, in part simply to enliven their respective

chapters in the story of American commerce. Both acknowledge that the subjects of their writing are potentially dull: Melville's narrator does "a snug business among rich men's bonds and mortgages and title-deeds" (14), requiring his scriveners to do work that is "dull, wearisome, and lethargic" (20), while Irving admits that his project involved "the trouble of rummaging among business papers, and of collecting and collating facts from amidst tedious and commonplace details" (vii). Both therefore use these mildly roguish characters to make the stories they tell more appealing to an audience looking to be jollied and entertained—an audience that Melville's narrator thinks of as being made up of "good-natured gentlemen" and "sentimental souls" (13) like himself.

Melville's narrator, then, uses Turkey and Nippers to help secure an audience of like-minded gentlemen for his narrative; Melville, on the other hand, uses them to foreground the issue of audience and to introduce into his story the subject of writing professionally, especially for an American audience. The occupation of the two characters is the copying of manuscripts, and the nicknames they go by are both terms used in the business of book production: many nineteenth-century editions were bound in "turkey," a kind of leather, and the automatic printing presses used "nippers" to hold page sheets in place.[35] The significance of these rather arcane allusions—both those to Irving's *Astoria* and those to the publishing business—is clarified by the presence of Bartleby, the silent man who refuses to play a part in the business of the narrator's office. Bartleby is the antithesis of all that the narrator and his patron, Astor, represent, and therefore of all that Irving celebrates in *Astoria*; he is neither competitive nor interested in money, and he clearly has no wish to win the approval of his own would-be patron, the narrator. He is a disturbing enigma whose story cannot be told, and who therefore has to be gotten out of the way so that the office business of America, especially the business of making money by the production of writing, can go on.

From Melville's perspective, Bartleby is the urban equivalent of Irving's western Indians, the people whose history was for Irving an enigma, whose lives were a "prolonged and all-besetting death," and whose inevitable disappearance Irving could only attribute to an innate "tendency to extinction" (227). Bartleby and the Indians must yield their place, on the land and in the written versions of history offered to an American audience, to those for whom a full and satisfactory biography can be written, men like John Jacob Astor.

Irving explains in the introduction to *Astoria* that Astor had suggested he write the book because "the true nature and extent of his enterprise and its national character and importance had never been understood" (vi). In attempting to make clear to his audience the full importance of Astor's career, Irving explains that those who pioneered in the search for gold and in the fur trade—Astor's business—had made possible the civilizing of the continent. "Without pausing on the borders, they have penetrated at once, in defiance of difficulties and dangers, to the heart of savage countries: laying open the hidden secrets of the wilderness; leading the way to remote regions of beauty and fertility that might have remained unexplored for ages" (13). This vast project in which, according to Irving, the pioneers of commerce have been gloriously successful, is structurally the same project the narrator sets himself in his dealings with Bartleby: to penetrate to what has been hidden, to reveal secrets, to release what is potential and then to appropriate it for the purposes of the American commercial enterprise. The narrator fails completely and, in spite of all his self-defensiveness, is ultimately willing to confess his failure and his frustration. Through his allusions to Irving—and to McKenney—Melville implies that the national project has also been a failure, to which the silent figure of the Indian, the unassimilated other, gives testimony. But Melville also implies that the successful American writer, the one whom the public validates and rewards, has always been and will continue to be the one who can simply banish the silently accusing other, mourn his melancholy fate, and continue to perpetuate the cheerful lie.

The narrator of "Bartleby" obviously struggles to save himself by clinging to the cheerful lie of unanimity and univocality; in Captain Delano of "Benito Cereno," Melville created a character whose "singularly undistrustful good nature" (47) allows him to maintain the same lie with only a minimum of struggle. Delano, the kindly American, saves himself psychologically through his habit of "drowning criticism in compassion" (58), choosing not to let the signs of conspiratorial intent he sees around him impinge on his benign, straightforward view of the world. As Eric Sundquist has said, Delano is "a virtual embodiment of repression" whose refusal to understand the complex situation on board the slave ship is a "psychologically and politically repressive act."[36] Both kinds of repression are necessary for Delano to retain his composure and his authority, and both can be expressed in a single act, but Melville suggests that the two impulses have different sources and require that Delano maintain two different self-images that might seem to be contradictory. The psychological repression, that allows him simply to put out of his mind any "imputation of malign evil in man" (47), requires Delano to think of himself as an innocent, a boy, whose instinct to trust in the good is *natural* and therefore cannot be ultimately deceiving. On the other hand, the political repression—the refusal to acknowledge that the blacks on the ship have either the will or the ingenuity to engineer a successful revolution against their white owners—requires that Delano think of himself as a father, a sympathetic superior who knows what is best for the vulnerable inferiors who have been placed in his charge.

At the moment when Delano begins to feel most threatened on the *San Dominick*, most "qualmish," he restores his equilibrium by calling up the image of himself as a boyish innocent:

> What, I, Amasa Delano—Jack of the Beach, as they called me when a lad—I, Amasa; the same that, duck-satchel in hand, used to paddle along the waterside to the school-house made from the old hulk;—I, little Jack of the Beach, that used to go berrying with cousin Nat and the rest; I to be murdered here at the ends of the earth, on board a haunted pirate-ship by a horrible Spaniard?—Too nonsensical to think of! Who would murder Amasa Delano? His conscience is clean. There is some one above. (77)

Delano's psychological maneuver works to get rid of the qualms by convincing him that it is still the schoolboy's world he inhabits, one in which private emotion is an accurate index to the real, external state of things. By thinking of himself as a boy, he can begin to see the world as "responsive to his own present feelings" (77), and they are blithely cheerful feelings.

Through Delano's wish to retain the conscience and the consciousness of the child, Melville seems to be deliberately testing out Emerson's contention at the beginning of "Nature" that the man who is in the right relation to his surroundings and to history is one "who has retained the spirit of infancy even into the era of manhood." Such a child-man, Emerson's newborn American, is capable of rising to the challenge Emerson extends to his generation:

> Our age is retrospective. It builds the sepulchres of the fathers. . . .
> Embosomed for a season in nature, whose floods of life stream around
> and through us, and invite us, by the powers they supply, to action
> proportioned to nature, why should we grope among the dry bones
> of the past, or put the living generation into masquerade out of its
> faded wardrobe? The sun shines today also.[37]

Delano is Emerson's child-man thoroughly ironized. On board the *San Dominick*, Delano is in the presence of the literal "dry bones" of the skeleton that serves as the ship's figurehead, and every action he observes is part of a complex and sinister "masquerade" expressly designed to conceal the truth from him. He does not penetrate the masquerade because he chooses not to be distrustful or suspicious, and even when the truth has been revealed through the shock of violence, Delano can still say, in a sunny echo of Emerson, that "the past is passed; why moralize upon it? Forget it. See, yon bright sun has forgotten it all, and the blue sea, and the blue sky; these have turned over new leaves" (116). Delano still wishes to be Jack of the Beach, the boy whose conviction of his own innocence cancels out whatever he might have learned from experience—personal or historical—about the potential for violence in a world where some are masters and some are slaves. In the duck-satchel that Jack of the Beach carries to school, there are evidently no relevant history books.

The other self-image, that of the benevolent and paternal superior, prompts Delano to "compassion" and "charity" (115) in his dealings with Benito Cereno and with the blacks on the ship. But his paternalism is not only grotesquely inappropriate to the situation on the *San Dominick*; it also leads him to near-fatal misreadings of the signs he sees there. He thinks of Benito Cereno, a man much younger than himself, not as a blithe lad protected, like himself, by his innocence, but as a young incompetent, subject to "infantile weakness" (65). The blacks, he knows, are "too stupid" to carry out a conspiracy; he thinks of them as naturally suited to be servants and happy in their servitude, because of their generic "docility arising from the unaspiring contentment of a limited mind" (75, 84). Their limitations make them easy to trust: "Captain Delano took to negroes, not philanthropically, but genially, just as other men to Newfoundland dogs" (84). His paternalism also allows him to hold onto his rather schoolmasterish reverence for order: he connects order with authority and virtue, disorderliness with vice.

By referring repeatedly to Delano as "the American," Melville makes it clear that he means him to be a representative figure, one whose repressions, evasions, and self-contradictions are part of what constitutes his Americanness. When Delano first comes aboard the slave ship, he is momentarily disoriented by the "strange costumes, gestures and faces" (50) he sees; to reorient himself, he quickly finds a way of nullifying the strangeness by mentally placing the blacks in a category familiar to most Americans—that of the tractable savage. In observing the blacks, he is most pleased by two things: their "good conduct," which gives him "humane satisfaction" (52), and their display of "naked nature," which prompts him to feel "gratified with their manners" (73). Confronted by Atufal, the gigantic black man in chains, Delano urges Benito Cereno to release him "in view of his general docility, as well as in some natural respect for his spirit" (63). Atufal, therefore, becomes for Delano the embodiment of his own two (Emersonian) self-images projected onto the other: he combines docility and spirit, civil behavior and naturalness, the reasonableness of the man and the spontaneity of the child.

Some of the details of the story also suggest that although Melville was primarily concerned with the potential for violence that he saw in the future for slaveholding America, he was also drawing on the history of violence that had resulted from the white culture's insistence that the American savages—the Indians—must add "docility" and "good conduct" to their natural spiritedness. Melville uses some of these details to connect his story with contemporary Indian-white conflicts in the western states and territories. At one point, for example, when Delano begins to feel "a dreamy inquietude, like that of one who alone on the prairie feels unrest from the repose of noon," he notices a Spanish sailor peering out from the rigging "like an Indian from behind a hemlock" (74). When the truth about the in-surrection is revealed and Delano's sailors are sent out to take the *San Dominick*, they are described as "fighting as troopers in the saddle," while the blacks on the ship "Indian-like, . . . hurtled their hatchets" (102, 101).

In some of the other details, Melville seems to be specifically recalling King Philip's War, that early conflict in which hundreds of "intractable" Indians were killed and many more were captured and subsequently sold as slaves. For instance, the real Amasa Delano, whose account of an insurrection on a slave ship Melville adapted for his story, came from Boston, while in Melville's story Delano's home is changed to Duxbury—which was also the home of Benjamin Church, the man who hunted down Philip and then wrote a history of the war. In his account, Church notes that he was accompanied on several of his forays against Philip by a Captain Dillano, whose name, according to one editor of Church's narrative, should properly have been spelled *Delano*.[38] Both Philip and Babo led a rebellion of nonwhites against whites, and were given the same treatment in defeat: their followers were killed or sent into slavery, while Philip and Babo themselves were both decapitated and their heads put on display in a public place.

These references extend the implications of Melville's story be-yond the issue of black slavery, as they deepen the layers of its irony. Captain Delano is an amiable and compassionate man who is pleased with his perception of himself as both an innocent boy and a generous father; he is also pleased with his comfortable perception of the dark-skinned other as one who combines spiritedness and docility. Delano explains his behavior on the *San Dominick* by attributing it to three sources—the guidance of Providence, his innate good nature, and his response to the immediate needs of the moment: " 'Yes, all is owing to Providence, I know; but the temper of my mind that morning was more than commonly pleasant, while the sight of so much suffering, more apparent than real, added to my good nature, compassion, and charity, happily interweaving the three' " (115). Melville suggests, however, that the interweaving Delano speaks of is neither happy nor genuinely spontaneous but that, instead, his attitude has actually been formed and nurtured by the peculiar circumstances of white America's historic relationship with the Indians. In Delano's reaction to those he perceives as uncivilized, we can see Melville's analysis of the two images of itself that white America has struggled to maintain in the eyes of the rest of the world: the youthful innocent and the wise father caring for his vulnerable and often misguided red children. To maintain the two images means, as Benito Cereno points out, that one cannot afford to have a memory. It also requires that one repress all awareness of those "enigmas and portents" (67) that can point toward a violent hatred hidden behind the other's mask of civility. And as in "Bartleby" and in *Moby-Dick*, the one who is best able to avoid a full understanding of what has happened, the one most adept at falling back on the uncritical use of a received discourse, is the one who survives to contribute his version to history, while those who do understand more fully—in this case, Benito Cereno and Babo—are destroyed.

In *The Confidence-Man*, Melville again set his story on a boat carrying "slaves, black, mulatto, quadroon," but this time the slaves make up only one small part of the heterogeneous group on the boat; there are also "mocassined squaws," "Sioux chiefs solemn as high-priests," and a long list of representatives of "all kinds of that multiform pilgrim species, man." These pilgrims are traveling together from St. Louis to New Orleans, and their presence on the boat allows the narrator to give an exuberant interpretation of the scene they present: "Here reigned the dashing and all-fusing spirit of the West, whose type is the Mississippi itself, which, uniting the streams of the most distant and opposite zones, pours them along, helter-skelter, in one cosmopolitan and confident tide" (6).

This paean to the Mississippi, as a symbol of the frontier spirit that unites the most diverse people and fuses them into a confident whole, at least echoes (if it does not directly borrow from) George Catlin's explanation of the importance of the river to the formation of the American character:

> The mighty Mississippi, however, the great and everlasting highway on which these people are for ever to intermingle their interests and manners, will effectually soften down those prejudices, and eventually result in an amalgamation of feelings and customs, from which this huge mass of population will take one new and general appellation. . . . It is here that the true character of the *American* is to be formed— here where the peculiarities and incongruities which detract from his true character are surrendered.[39]

If Melville is calling on Catlin here, however, he is clearly doing so only to mock Catlin's earnest optimism and his belief that the term *American* signifies a unitary "true character." On board his *Fidèle* there are *only* peculiarities and incongruities, and the only real unity is to be found in the "cosmopolitan and confident tide" of rhetoric that the confidence man evokes from the passengers. Late in the novel, Frank Goodman (the confidence man in one of his avatars) and Charlie Noble agree that "the voice of the people is the voice of truth" (142); that statement makes a deeply ironic sense for the microcosm of the *Fidèle*, where the talking goes on all day long, and where the voices of the talkers merge in a version of the truth that the silence of the other passengers—including the slaves and the Indians—covertly undermines for the reader.

Melville calls our attention to what is *not* said in the very opening scene of the novel, with the introduction of the "lamb-like" (4), mute stranger who carries a slate on which he writes the apostle Paul's descriptions of charity. His silent reminders of the Christian definition of charity are quickly replaced by the vocal solicitations of the man in gray, who is (or pretends to be) a kind of professional charity man, looking for contributions to the Widow and Orphan Asylum for the Seminoles. When he succeeds in getting a donation from the Episcopal clergyman on board, the man in gray offers the clergyman an explanation: "And now let me give you a little history of our asylum, and the providential way in which it was started" (29). The chapter ends with that sentence, however, so that the reader hears none of the story of the founding of the Seminole asylum. Most readers in 1857 would have known at least the outlines of the story, since they would surely remember the Seminole War of 1835–1842, in which the U.S. government created a great many Seminole widows and orphans, who were then transported across the same river that the *Fidèle* of the novel is steaming down. The long Seminole War was a source of national frustration and eventually of national embarrassment—so much so that George Catlin recommended that Americans would do well to remove it from their collective consciousness:

> The world will pardon me for saying no more of this inglorious war, for it will be seen that I am too near the end of my book, to afford the requisite space; and as an American citizen, I would pray, amongst thousands of others, that all books yet to be made, might have as good an excuse for leaving it out.[40]

Melville's deliberate omission of the account of the founding of the Seminole Widow and Orphan Asylum may be a direct response to Catlin's wish that the story of the Seminole War be left out of American books. But whether he meant an allusion here or not, his point is made: in this microcosm of midcentury America, where the dominant voices agree that "whatever else one may be, he must be genial or he is nothing" (154), no speaker can discuss openly such episodes as a messy seven-year war of extermination against the Indians. To do so would be to take himself out of this genial American conversation, and thus—in Melville's terms—to become nothing.

The Confidence-Man also includes the section that Melville's critics have tended to fasten on as most revealing of his attitude toward Indians: the long conversation between Charlie Noble and Frank Goodman on the metaphysics of Indian-hating (chaps. 25–28).[41] The primary source for this section has been identified as Judge James

Hall's chapter on Indian-hating in his *Sketches of History, Life, and Manners, in the West*. Melville quoted and paraphrased freely from Hall, but there are other allusions in the section that indicate that he intended a wider comment on white American writing on the Indians in general. He calls up Cooper, for example, in Noble's description of the frontiersman as a "Pathfinder" (126) and of the Indian-hater as "a Leather-stocking Nemesis" (130). Robert Montgomery Bird's *Nick of the Woods*, the story of a misanthropic Indian-hater, is introduced in Goodman's comment that Hall's example of the Indian-hater, John Moredock, "would seem a Moredock of Misanthrope Hall—the Woods" (122), and Noble's mention of "the wigwams and the cabins" seems a direct allusion to William Gilmore Simms's *The Wigwam and the Cabin*. Goodman also reels off a list of Indians— Pocahontas, Massasoit, Philip, Tecumseh, Red-Jacket, Logan—all of whom had been extensively written about, and thoroughly mythologized, by the middle of the nineteenth century. Goodman acknowledges the mythologizing when he prefaces his list by protesting that Indians are "one of the finest of the primitive races, possessed of many heroic virtues" (122).

At the end of his list of individual Indian heroes Goodman mentions the Five Nations, the Iroquois confederacy whose history was first written by Cadwallader Colden in 1727. Colden's history is particularly relevant to the discussion of Indian-hating on the *Fidèle* in two ways. First, Colden's description of the Indians as an "extreamly Revengeful" people who will do anything to "gratifie that Devouring Passion, which seems to gnaw their Souls, and gives them no ease till it is satisfied"[42] attributes to the Indians exactly the characteristic of obsessive vengefulness that Noble, following Hall, gives to the Indian-hater. And second, Noble's story of the five white cousins who made a treaty with the Indian Mocmohoc, and then were killed through Mocmohoc's sly reinterpretation of the terms of the treaty, reverses the long history of the Five Nations' various betrayals by the French and English colonial officials with whom they made their own treaties.

Melville's reversing of these two particular points in Colden's history is characteristic of the procedure of the whole Indian-hating section. Near the end of their conversation, Goodman tells Noble that "our sentiments agree so, that were they written in a book, whose was whose, few but the nicest critics might determine" (137). In *this* book, Melville argues, by implication, that the characteristics of Indian and Indian-hater—as each has been confidently defined by white writers—can be made to agree so well that one might in fact be substituted for the other. Noble's story of Moredock includes the argument that as a backwoodsman, Moredock was part of "the vanguard of conquering civilization" (126), and as a man who renounced personal ambition, he provided a good example of the Christian virtue of eschewing "the pomps and vanities of the world" (135). Noble, that is, attempts to establish that the white man is distinguished from the Indian because he is a Christian and a civilizer, but his story actually demonstrates that Moredock, a man of a "sultry and tragical brown" complexion (134), is indistinguishable from the Indians he hates.

Moredock's skills as a man of the woods, according to Hall and Noble, are those of the stereotypical Indian of white novels and history books:

> As an athlete, he had few equals; as a shot, none; in single combat, not to be beaten. Master of that woodland-cunning enabling the adept to subsist where the tyro would perish, and expert in all those arts by which an enemy is pursued for weeks, perhaps months, without once suspecting it, he kept to the forest. The solitary Indian that met him, died. When a number was descried, he would either secretly pursue their track for some chance to strike at least one blow; or if, while thus engaged, he himself was discovered, he would elude them by superior skill. (133–34)

Moredock's domestic accomplishments and virtues are also those that white writers were likely to remark among Indians: he was concerned for the safety of his people, good to his wife and children, hospitable, courteous, and a skilled singer and storyteller. Noble finds the combination of these traits "apparently self-contradicting, certainly curious" (134) in the white man, whereas he finds inconsistency only to be expected in the Indians. In dealing with Indians, he says, one must be prepared to find that "those red men who are the greatest sticklers for the theory of Indian virtue, and Indian loving-kindness, are sometimes the arrantest horse-thieves and tomahawk-ers among them" (128). By pointing out the contradictions in the Indian character, Noble is repeating a point that was made often by nineteenth-century white writers. For example, in the following account, taken from an 1843 review of Stone's *Life of Brant*, the reviewer might as easily have been describing the Indian-hater Moredock as the Indian Brant:

> In Brant, barbarism and civilization evinced a strong and singular contest. He was at one moment a savage, and at another a civilian, at one moment cruel, and at another humane; and he exhibited, through-out all the heroic period of his career, a constant vacillation and strug-gle between good and bad, noble and ignoble feelings, and, as one or the other got the mastery, he was an angel of mercy, or a demon of destruction. In this respect, his character does not essentially vary from that which has been found to mark the other leading red men who, from Philip to Osceola, have appeared on the stage of action. . . . The fact that he could use the pen, supplied no insuperable motives against his wielding the war club. His tomahawk and his Testament lay on the same shelf.[43]

Francis Parkman was to use this same emphasis on contradictions as the basis of his analysis of Indian character in *The Conspiracy of Pontiac* (1851); while the Indian might seem inscrutable, Parkman argues, "yet to the eye of rational observation there is nothing un-intelligible in him" as long as the interpreter begins with the under-standing that "he is full . . . of contradictions."[44]

For the reader familiar with the tradition in which Judge Hall wrote—a tradition that made it possible for Hall to write as he did—the discussion of Indian-hating is not a serious philosophical medi-tation or an allegory of good and evil but a thoroughly ironic pastiche made up of the confident assertions of white writers who professed to understand the vast difference between being an Indian and hating Indians. The number of Melville's allusions in the section is itself a reminder that the popular Hall constructed his frontier stories and sketches out of bits and pieces taken from other writers; among his many sources (some acknowledged and some not) were Washington Irving, Charles Fenno Hoffman, Lewis Cass, Henry Rowe Schoolcraft, William H. Keating, and John Tanner. In scrambling his own allusions and allowing them to reveal their inherent contradictions, Melville was not so much defending the Indian as he was attacking the complacency of contemporary writers and readers about the distinction between the civilized person and the savage—the distinction on which so much of the justification for white America's displacement of the Indians rested.

The Confidence-Man is, as Carolyn Karcher has said, "Melville's most powerful indictment of nineteenth-century America" as a country that was "enslaving and massacring its nonwhite citizens while posing as a political and religious haven."[45] There is no enslaving or massacring going on aboard the *Fidèle*, but there is constant verbal posing, and there are reminders of the silent blacks and Indians who are present on the boat *and* in the text of the novel. Charlie Noble articulates one good motto for all the talkers of the *Fidèle*: "If Truth don't speak through the people, it never speaks at all; so I heard one say" (142). In this microcosm of midcentury democratic America, only the language of confidence and geniality, the homogenizing, recirculated discourse that feeds on itself ("so I heard one say"), can contribute to the Truth; the alternative truth, tangibly embodied in the silent blacks and Indians, "never speaks at all."

3 | *Saving the Family: Hawthorne, Child, and Sedgwick*

IN 1833 THE Massachussetts lawyer and sometime politician Rufus Choate delivered an address in Salem on the subject of "The Importance of Illustrating New-England History by a Series of Romances Like the Waverley Novels." The writer who could produce such a series would, Choate predicted, make the "heroic age" of American history "for the first time familiar, intelligible, and interesting to the mass of the reading community."[1] Of the New England subjects that had already been treated by the historians, Choate singled out two that he saw as especially amenable to revisioning by the writer of romance: the specific crisis of King Philip's War and the more general "moral phenomenon" of "the old Puritan character" (328, 333). Although Choate was willing to grant that the historians had already given these subjects a generally accurate treatment, he was not willing to accept their versions as sufficient or complete:

> History shows you prospects by starlight, or at best by the waning moon. Romantic fiction, as Scott writes it, does not create a new heaven and a new earth; but it just pours the brightness of noonday over the earth and sky. . . . [In romance], you see the best of everything,—all that is grand and beautiful of nature, all that is brilliant in achievement, all that is magnanimous in virtue, all that is sublime in self-sacrifice; and you see a great deal more of which history shows you nothing. (341)

In Choate's view, then, the American writer of romance could per-
form a valuable service to the country by giving the reading public
both a body of indigenous literature that might compete with the
novels of Scott and, at the same time, a new version of colonial
history that might become a source of national pride. The sunlight
of romance, Choate suggests, because it reveals only "the best of
everything" and deliberately obscures all that "chills, shames, and
disgusts us" (339), might help to eliminate the shadowy moral ambiguities and failures that are part of the documented record of colonial history, especially the record of Puritan conflicts with the
Indians.

Since Choate does not mention any of the literary treatments of
Puritan-Indian conflicts that had already been produced by 1833, it
is not clear whether he simply had not noticed them or whether he
was dissatisfed with the treatment that the American "heroic age"
had received thus far.[2] Either way, his remarks introduce a useful
context for considering the attractions of colonial history as a subject
for imaginative writers in the first half of the nineteenth century—
especially since Choate's speech suggests that by 1833 even some of
the politicians were beginning to look to the fiction writers for help
in reaffirming that the entire course of American history, when seen
from the right angle and in the right light, could be perceived as a
record of "achievement," "virtue," and "self-sacrifice."

If we remember that Choate gave his speech only three years
after passage of the Indian Removal Act, one year after Black Hawk's
War, and while the divisive debates on the fate of the Cherokees
were still in progress, then it is easier for us to recognize the important subtext of his speech and thus to understand his reasons both
for urging American writers in 1833 to take up the specific subject
of colonial conflicts with the Indians and for advising them about
how best to handle the subject. In recommending a reconstruction
of colonial history, Choate is offering a way of making that early
history more continuous with the political realities of 1833. (He is
also, and not too incidentally, urging the recognition that New England is still the section that has the most representative history, that
is the appropriate source of moral guidance for the rest of the coun-

try, and that is likely to produce the most responsible and accomplished literature.) Choate recommends the Wampanoag chief Philip, for example, as a figure with the potential for becoming a tragic hero in the new American canon; Philip determined his own fate by continuing to wage a fierce war on the white colonists, Choate says, even though "the terrible truth had at length flashed upon the Indian chief, that the presence of civilization, even of humane, peaceful, and moral civilization, was incompatible with the existence of Indians" (336–37). Similarly, he recommends a new and more dramatically interesting reading of the Puritans, whose descriptions of themselves in their own histories might make them seem woodenly inhumane and intolerant to a contemporary audience. The romance writer, Choate says, can help American readers understand that the Puritan character

> was developed, disciplined, and perfected for a particular day and a particular duty. When that day was ended and that duty done, it was dissolved again into its elements, and disappeared among the common forms of humanity, apart from which it had acted and suffered. . . . (333–34)

What might seem like uncalled-for cruelty in the Puritan treatment of the Indians, in other words, can be interpreted as a temporary and necessary response to an unpleasant duty—a duty required for the preservation of "humane, peaceful, and moral civilization." If Choate's audience could be made to understand the Puritans' conflicts with the Indians in this way, then they might better understand a more immediate issue, that is, that the decision to remove the Indians from the white America of the 1830s was not so much a form of political and economic expediency with local benefits as a painful moral duty for the nation, requiring a temporary resurgence of the old Puritan firmness of character.

Choate's speech is naive both in its definition of romance as necessarily sunny and in its assumptions about the kind of power that the writer of romances can have over the political judgments of the public.[3] This naiveté, however, seems deliberate; Choate is clearly more concerned to promote good feeling than good writing. What he calls for is, in Lawrence Buell's words, a form of "benign censorship" of the historical record.[4] From our perspective, therefore, the speech is more interesting as political propaganda than as a notable document in literary history. On the other hand, although Choate may seem especially heavy-handed in his manipulation of historical material to make it serve the needs of the present moment (as he interprets those needs), his urge to revise the interpretations of American history to make them more conformable to the present mood and objectives of America is an urge shared by many of his contemporaries, including some whose hands are much lighter and defter than Choate's.

In the remainder of this chapter, I want to examine three novels that take aspects of Puritan history as their subjects—Lydia Maria Child's *Hobomok* (1824), Catherine Sedgwick's *Hope Leslie* (1827), and Nathaniel Hawthorne's *The Scarlet Letter* (1850)—and suggest the ways in which their treatments of seventeenth-century America are determined by the writers' concerns for the present and future of nineteenth-century America. More specifically, since all three of these novels have female protagonists, I want to illustrate the extent to which each writer's responses to the nineteenth-century versions of both "the Indian question" and "the woman question" determine her or his portrayal of the relationship between the early colonists and the Indians. Although two of the novels were written before passage of the Removal Act and one was written well after removal was an accomplished fact, all three share an implicit assumption that the destiny of the Indians appears to be extinction, or at least a slow fade into silence and invisibility. They differ significantly, however, in their accounting for the fate of the Indians and in the kinds of analogies they draw between the Indians' struggle with Puritan patriarchy and the struggle of white women with nineteenth-century American patriarchy.

All three writers make it clear that although they have done their homework carefully and intend to respect the historical record, their real object in writing is to do just what Choate asked of fiction writers: to offer contemporary readers a new perspective on the old record and a new way of interpreting it. Sedgwick announces in her preface that the allusions to actual people and events in *Hope Leslie* are there only because she found them "convenient" to her real purpose, which is to illuminate "not the history, but the character of the times."[5] In the preface to *Hobomok*, Child attributes the authorship of her novel to a fictitious (male) writer who describes the book as an attempt not to reconstruct but only to reanimate the familiar and by now lifeless histories of New England in order to make them attractive to a contemporary reader: "barren and uninteresting as New England history is, I feel there is enough connected with it, to rouse the dormant energies of my soul. . . . "[6] Similarly, in "The Custom House," Hawthorne traces the origin of his novel to his energizing discovery of the scarlet A, a neglected "relic" of New England Puritanism that had been relegated to the dusty lumber room of history.[7]

Both Child and Sedgwick, furthermore, indicate that their new interpretations of the past have been made possible by the presence of a new kind of audience, one that has only recently come into being. Child reminds her readers that they, unlike the Puritans they are reading about, live in an "enlightened and liberal age" (6), and Sedgwick specifically addresses her book to "the liberal philanthropist" and the "enlightened and accurate observer of human nature" (6). Such readers should be able to understand the peculiar limitations of New England Puritanism, both writers imply, precisely because they are intellectually and morally so distanced from it.

Hawthorne, on the other hand, makes no such distinction between new readers and old characters, nor does he presuppose any liberal-mindedness on the part of his readers; the audience he projects in "The Custom-House" is only "a friend, a kind and apprehensive, though not the closest friend, [who] is listening to our talk" (35). He even goes out of his way to suggest that he has nothing to say that would appeal to the modern philanthropist. This suggestion is made obliquely in "The Custom House" through the heavily ironic portrait of "the General," a man with whom Hawthorne says he could manage only a "slight" communication (52). After speculating

about what the General must have been like in the days when he
acquired his reputation for military valor, Hawthorne concludes with
a summation of the present General, the man of the Custom House:

> What I saw in him . . . were the features of stubborn and ponderous
> endurance, which might well have amounted to obstinacy in his earlier
> days; of integrity, that, like most of his other endowments, lay in a
> somewhat heavy mass, and was just as unmalleable and unmanageable
> as a ton of iron ore; and of benevolence, which, fiercely as he led the
> bayonets on at Chippewa or Fort Erie, I take to be of quite as genuine
> a stamp as what actuates any or all the polemical philanthropists of
> the age. (53)

The benevolence of contemporary "polemical philanthropists," Hawthorne implies here, is as leaden and unconsidered a quality as is the
lumpishness that passes for integrity in the General. Between the
author of *The Scarlet Letter* and the modern philanthropist there can
be, apparently, only slight communication.

   These representations of audience in the three novels provide one
important index of each writer's understanding of the direction and
velocity of change in American culture. Hawthorne clearly distrusts
the notion that the nature of the political and social realities of the
present can be significantly changed by taking a more liberal view of
them. The opening chapter of *The Scarlet Letter* specifically invites
the modern reformer to compare his (or, more appropriately, her)
vision of a "Utopia of human virtue and happiness" (75) with the
doomed utopianism of the Puritans, while the closing chapters demonstrate, through the chastened Hester's resumption of her bleak life
in repressive Boston, that genuine enlightenment consists in knowing
that social change always comes slowly and is never brought about
by the will, or even the suffering, of a few impatient individuals.
Both Child and Sedgwick, on the other hand, accept without question
the view that the intellectual and psychological narrowness of Puritan
culture has given way to the enlightened liberalism of the nineteenth
century and that the change has been brought about by the actions
of people who recognized injustice and refused to submit to it. As
Sedgwick puts it,

> The character of man, and the institutions of society, are yet very far
> from their possible and destined perfection. Still, how far is the present
> age in advance of that which drove reformers to a dreary wilderness!—
> of that which hanged quakers!—of that which condemned to death,
> as witches, innocent, unoffending old women! But it is unnecessary
> to heighten the glory of our risen day by comparing it with the pre-
> ceding twilight. (16)

Furthermore, both Child and Sedgwick find the primary reason for
the steady progress of American culture in the gradual demolition of
patriarchal control through the efforts of enlightened individuals, not
only control of social institutions but also of the written interpretations of those institutions. If the male historians of the seventeenth
century—the Mathers, Winthrops, and Hubbards—were limited by
their need to reaffirm Calvinist theology, including its unofficial valorizing of male supremacy, the female novelists of the nineteenth
century are, according to Child and Sedgwick, definitely not so limited. The female perspective, which both writers associate with imagination and "feeling," provides a corrective to the intellectual
repressiveness of patriarchal history making *and* history writing.

In retrospect, we can see how strongly the attitudes of Child and
Sedgwick toward the possibilities of reform were influenced by the
Unitarian movement that was attracting the attention of most New
England intellectuals in the first third of the century, and converting
many of them. Both women had strong connections to Unitarian
intellectual circles: Child wrote *Hobomok* while she was living with
her brother, a Unitarian minister, and Sedgwick joined a Unitarian
congregation in 1821, six years before she wrote *Hope Leslie*. Their
novels attest to the enthusiasm with which both women embraced
the new "Liberal Christianity," which aimed at replacing the Calvinist doctrines of natural depravity and special election with an emphasis on the ability of the individual to be guided toward the good
by the light of reason and intuition. Most important, both fully
accepted the major secular ramification of Unitarian theology: the
premise that human society is as susceptible of improvement as is
the individual, and that progress toward social harmony can be
achieved through rational inquiry and the enlightened reform of old

attitudes and institutions. In rejecting the Calvinist theory that "there is a class of sinners whose strivings toward a good life must forever be fruitless,"[8] the Unitarians also rejected the notion that there were classes of people whose efforts to share the benefits of social progress must likewise be fruitless. In their novels, Child and Sedgwick are both able to use their female protagonists to support the argument for the value of social reform. Working backward from their own circumstances in the early years of the nineteenth century, when women (like Child and Sedgwick) are sufficiently liberated to debate ideas with men and publish novels that revise male-transmitted history, they can argue that the changed status of women is the result of a process of reform begun nearly two hundred years before by the small rebellions of a few spirited and intelligent women against the Puritan patriarchy. Thus they can urge the continued effort to bring women into full equality and, at the same time, to revise the Puritan view of women as intellectually weak and politically impotent.

If contemporary circumstances made it possible for Child and Sedgwick to begin rewriting the history of women in America, however, they made it very difficult to rewrite, in any significant way, the history of Indians in America. Both women clearly wish to revise the Puritan historians' representations of Indians as devilish savages and brutes. Just as important, both women implicitly assert the claim of the female novelist, whose fictional domain is still largely limited to the places that women and children inhabit, to invent Indian characters who can be brought out of the woods—the domain of the male novelists—and into the domestic place. In this regard, both women can be seen as at least tentatively attempting to dislodge the categorical distinctions that had, by the early nineteenth century, separated gender out from issues or questions that might be termed political. As Anita Levy points out, "If gender seems to be located with the female in the household [in the nineteenth century], then race and class belong to the male domains of political and natural or cultural history, respectively."[9] But for Child and Sedgwick, the project of merging issues of gender and race means only that they experiment with moving their Indian characters, for a short time, into the privileged domain of the white woman. Both writers link their Indian characters to their white female characters, as sharers of a sensibility that instinctively values "the voice of nature" over the rigidity of Calvinist dogma and therefore as common victims of the bigotry of Puritan males: Sedgwick's white heroine takes the side of the Indian woman Magawisca in opposing the Puritan elders, risking her life to help Magawisca escape from prison, and Child's heroine, defying her Puritan father, actually marries the Indian Hobomok and bears his son. Yet both writers have to acknowledge that if the active rebellion of colonial women eventually made it possible for enlightened white women like themselves to thrive, and write, in the nineteenth century, the rebellion of their Indian counterparts led only to their silencing and their exclusion from the progressive culture of nineteenth-century America. The alliance between Indians (of both sexes) and white women, a fantasized alliance that is at the heart of both their novels, disintegrates in the face of historical realities.

The virtual absence of Indians from the New England of the 1820s, and the widespread public conviction that their presence anywhere in the eastern United States was an obstacle to the natural progress of American civilization, meant that although Child and Sedgwick might attempt to revise the Puritan characterizations of Indians, they could not reinstate the Indians in the trajectory of American history as easily as they could reinstate women; all they could do was try to account for the Indians' decline. In the course of trying to manage that accounting, ironically, both end up affirming an argument that was almost as hoary by the 1820s as the argument for male supremacy—the argument that the Indian was the "child of nature," a noble and sympathetic child to be sure, but nevertheless incapable of moving beyond the infantile state of unquestioning loyalty to his or her own patriarchs. The white heroines of these novels defy their fathers in attaching themselves to the Indians, but the Indian characters (male or female) will not, or cannot, defy their own fathers. For the Indian characters, deference to the patriarch *is* natural. They are therefore trapped in a kind of perpetual childhood, and so must be left behind while the young white women continue to grow in independence, drawing the rest of America on toward its full and healthy maturity.

In *Hobomok*, Child presents her heroine, Mary Conant, as the embodiment of all that the Puritan males find sinful or frivolous. Mary has a "poetic imagination" that is especially responsive to "the influence of nature" (91); this romantic, spontaneous side of Mary draws her into friendship with the Indian Hobomok,[10] whose conversation offers her a welcome alternative to the sober theological and political debates that make up most of the conversation among the men of Puritan Salem. The "untutored" Hobomok (who speaks almost entirely in metaphors) is a good storyteller; as he talks, Mary listens with fascination to his "descriptions of the Indian nations, glowing as they were in the brief, figurative language of nature" (84). But Mary is also bright and intellectually ambitious as well as imaginative, and therefore attracted to the Oxford-educated Englishman Charles Brown. For Child, the chief sign of Charles's intelligence is that he refuses to give up his Anglicanism and join the Puritan congregation, even though this refusal turns the rest of the men of Salem, including Mary's father, against him. Charles almost welcomes his ostracism; most of the Salem Puritans are "so far below his intellectual standard, that nothing could have saved them from his contempt, save the strong bond of religious unity; and under no circumstances, and in no situation whatever, could Brown have been a Puritan" (69). Mary's Calvinist father first forbids Charles to visit Mary, and then is instrumental in getting him banished from Salem altogether.

Mary's loneliness after Charles's departure from Salem is compounded by the death of her mother and the marriage of her one close female friend. With only her stern, emotionally distant father and the other members of the Puritan congregation as companions, Mary grows "more and more weary of the loneliness of unreciprocated intellect" (91). She sustains herself by relying on Charles's promise to return and take her back with him to England, until news reaches her that his ship has sunk in a storm, apparently leaving no survivors. In her grief she turns to her father, but Mr. Conant "did as he too often had done—stifled the voice of nature, and hid all his better feelings beneath the cold mask of austerity" (119). This rebuff from her father drives the desperate Mary to the one person on whom she knows she can rely for sympathy and understanding:

> There was a chaos in Mary's mind. . . . What now had life to offer? If she went to England, those for whom she most wished to return, were dead. If she remained in America, what communion could she have with those around her? Even Hobomok, whose language was brief, figurative, and poetic, and whose nature was unwarped by the artifices of civilized life, was far preferable to them. She remembered the idolatry he had always paid her, and in the desolation of the moment, she felt as if he was the only being in the wide world who was left to love her. (121)

Mary impulsively offers to marry Hobomok, and he eagerly accepts. They are married in an Indian ceremony, and Mary settles into his wigwam, where she expects to remain forever.

Mary's decision to marry Hobomok is treated rather hurriedly, but the reader has been prepared for it by the opening scenes of the novel. There, we see the young Mary sneaking out of her father's house at night and performing a private, girlish ritual in the moonlight. Drawing a circle on the ground, she walks around it three times, chanting a sort of incantation: "Whoe'er my bridegroom is to be, / Step in the circle after me" (13). To her surprise, Hobomok suddenly springs out of the darkness and into the center of the circle. He explains that he is on his way to the Spirit Rocks to make an offering to the "Manitto" (14); as they talk, they are joined by Charles Brown, who explains that he has dreamed Mary was in trouble and has come to reassure himself that she is safe. Mary's moonlight ritual, outside her father's house, has therefore summoned to her the two men who represent those two aspects of her nature—imagination and intellectual curiosity—that have been most repressed by the Puritan patriarchy. This interpretation of the ritual, however, occurs only to the reader and not to Mary; all she takes away from the strange experience is the conviction that her future has now been foretold and fixed, even if she does not fully understand the prediction. " 'I suppose I must submit to whatever is fore-ordained for me,' " she tells her friend Sally. Her girlish superstitiousness has, therefore, led her to take what is, ironically, an essentially Calvinist stance, submitting herself to a fate that, she is willing to assume, has been supernaturally determined.

When Mary decides to marry Hobomok, she justifies the decision to herself by falling back on this same fatalistic sense that her destiny is not within her own control. Her extraordinary action in "choosing the company of savages" is a sign, Child says, that Mary has "sunk under the stupefying influence of an ill directed belief in the decrees of heaven, and the utter fruitlessness of all endeavor" (122). Evidently Mary has soaked up enough Calvinism to complement her susceptibility to superstition, and the result is a rash, thoughtless decision that completely severs her from home and community. During the three years of the marriage, Hobomok is a devoted companion who cares for Mary as lovingly as he tends the son who is born to them. Child makes it clear, however, that because he is an Indian, Hobomok can never be more than a sort of older protective playmate for Mary; he is the gentle friend of her childhood, and her marriage to him is unnatural, preventing her from assuming her natural place as a mature white woman, living among her own kind:

> Kind as Hobomok was, and rich as she found his uncultivated mind in native imagination, still the contrast between him and her departed lover, would often be remembered with sufficient bitterness. Beside this, she knew that her own nation looked upon her as lost and degraded; and, what was far worse, her own heart echoed back the charge. (135)

Hobomok is a good Indian, according to Child, but his marriage to Mary, because she is white, is a bad marriage, and she is "degraded" by it.

Predictably, Charles Brown reappears at the close of the novel, having survived the shipwreck after all and endured three years of captivity somewhere on the coast of Africa (as Mary has endured her three-year captivity in marriage to an Indian). When he and Hobomok meet, the Indian husband knows immediately that he must relinquish Mary to his white rival: " '[T]he heart of Mary,' " he admits to Brown, " 'is not with the Indian.' " It would be best for him, Hobomok says, to " 'go far off among some of the red men in the west' " (139), leaving Mary to the care of her white lover. Charles gallantly protests that he cannot take Hobomok's family away from him, but Hobomok is resolute:

> "The purpose of an Indian is seldom changed. . . . My tracks will soon be seen far beyond the back-bone of the Great Spirit. For Mary's sake I have borne the hatred of the Yengees, the scorn of my tribe, and the insults of my enemy. And now, I will be buried among strangers, and none shall black their faces for the unknown chief. . . . Ask Mary to pray for me—that when I die, I may go to the Englishman's God, where I may hunt beaver with little Hobomok, and count my beavers for Mary." (140)

Without seeing Mary or his son again, the "high-souled child of the forest" abruptly walks off into the hills "and forever passed away from New England" (141).

This ending to the novel is both sentimental and formulaic, but the plot requires such an ending, with its infantilizing of Hobomok, because Child's interpretation of the history of the Indians in America is itself thoroughly sentimental. The Indians, according to her parable, were the friends of young America who provided a healthy corrective to the gloomy and dictatorial piety of the Puritan fathers. Their most important contribution was their encouragement of what Child sees as the feminization of the country: they offered the children of the Puritans, especially the daughters, living models of the spontaneous and imaginative life, the life of "feeling," and they helped to nurture in the impressionable daughters a religious attitude based on instinctive reverence rather than on received dogma. For all of this, enlightened Americans, especially women, ought to be grateful. But the Indians were children themselves, albeit old ones, who could not be expected to keep pace with the energy and vitality of the new white nation, significantly figured as the "daughter" of England in Child's image, who was "blushing into life with all the impetuosity of youthful vigor" (100). For the good of everyone in

America, including the Indians, these old children must voluntarily remove themselves out of the way of the sturdy white growth and seek their own kind in the West, trusting that the Christian God will reunite them with their white friends in the hereafter. For the white heroine, the separation from her Indian companion is a necessary part of the painful process of maturing; she begins to come of age only when she frees herself from both the tyrannical white father and her own regressive wish to live in the Indian's perpetual childhood.

In sending Hobomok off to his silent fate in the West, Child seems to suggest that removal of the Indians from the white America of the 1820s may be one sad but necessary solution to the problem of racial incompatibility. However, she also suggests another solution, through her brief summary of the life of the half-breed child, the son of Mary and Hobomok. The child, whom Mary names Charles Hobomok Conant, is reared in Salem by Mary and her new white husband, Charles Brown. The boy grows to become "a distinguished graduate at Cambridge; and when he left that infant university, he departed to finish his studies in England. His father was seldom spoken of; and by degrees his Indian appellation was silently omitted" (150). This small success story introduces the option of assimilating the Indians into white culture through education and the gradual erasing of the Indian's ties—even the tie of a name—to his native culture. However, this second option, which as Child's most recent editor has pointed out, "amounts to cultural genocide,"[11] works only in a very special case: the boy is only half Indian to begin with, and he is transplanted from one culture to another before he is three years old.

Child wrote *Hobomok* in 1824, when she was only twenty-two and when the Indian removal program was still only a possibility. As she grew older and as the removal theory was translated into official policy and then into military action, Child shifted from theorizing in fiction about the Indians' future to more direct attacks on the government's policies. Her posthumous reputation has come to rest on her almost lifelong work as an abolitionist and advocate of women's rights, but her concern for the rights of blacks and women only merged with, rather than eclipsing, her concern for the rights of Indians. In November of 1859 she wrote to John Brown, then in prison, "What is in store for us, I know not. But we are indeed a guilty nation. Guilty toward the Indians, toward the negroes, toward all that are weak and within our power."[12] In 1868 she published *An Appeal for the Indians*, in which she urged white America to recognize that "our relations with the red and black members of the human family have been one almost unvaried history of violence and fraud." And yet, even after more than forty years of close attention to the violent and often baroque realities of Indian-white relations in America, Child was still committed to the same general conception of those relations that had informed the sentimental novel she wrote at the age of twenty-two. Her chief object in *An Appeal* was to demonstrate that Indian nature was also human nature, and that the Indians were capable of gradual assimilation into white culture (that is, capable of "civilization") through proper education and a system of rewards to encourage them to abandon their traditional customs and languages. Most significantly, Child still held fast to her image of the Indians as blocked children: "How *ought* we to view the peoples who are less advanced than ourselves? Simply as younger members of the same great human family, who need to be protected, instructed and encouraged, till they are capable of appreciating and sharing all our advantages."[13] This "view" is exactly the one that had produced the fantasy of the young Charles Hobomok's transformation into Charles Conant, Harvard graduate, and the corresponding fantasy of the sad fate of his father, the old child who was incapable of assimilation into "the great human family."

Three years after Child published *Hobomok*, Catherine Sedgwick followed with her own attempt to further the liberation of colonial history—including its portrayal of the Indians as less than fully human creatures—from the grip of the Puritan historians. Like Child's novel, Sedgwick's *Hope Leslie* is a self-consciously femininist revision of male-transmitted history that attributes the present intellectual enlightenment of New England to the small rebellions of Puritan women against the domination of men. Sedgwick also links her white heroine, Hope Leslie, to an Indian character, but this time the Indian is another young woman, named Magawisca.[14] Sedgwick may have learned from the outraged response of some critics to the white-Indian marriage in *Hobomok* (the reviewer for the *North American Review* had called the marriage "revolting")[15] that the liberalism of the reading public still had its limits. Her novel does include a mixed marriage, but this time the partners are the white heroine's sister and the Indian heroine's brother, both of whom are weaker and more irresponsible than their older sisters. Furthermore, Sedgwick is careful to make it clear that Hope's sister, Faith, is a hopelessly dependent child whose choice of an Indian husband is one sign of her unwillingness to grow up. The older and wiser sisters, Hope and Magawisca, are both disturbed by the marriage; Hope's reaction, like that of the reviewer of *Hobomok*, is "an unthought-of revolting of nature" (227).

Sedgwick is also more attentive to the specific historical context of her story than Child is to hers, and more insistent that the repressiveness and violence of the period are directly attributable to the fact that it was an "age of undisputed masculine supremacy" (16). Significantly, however, her dominating males are not all Puritans, although she suggests that the Puritan theology provided men with a very useful way of reinforcing "the duty of unqualified obedience from the wife to the husband, her appointed lord and master; a duty that it was left to modern heresy to dispute" (144). Most of the women in the book are subjected to some form of captivity or imprisonment by men: Hope's English mother was literally captured by her own Anglican father as she and her lover were about to elope and join the Protestant dissenters in America; Magawisca was taken captive by white colonists as a child and sent to work as a servant in Hope's foster family, and is later imprisoned by the Puritan magistrates because they suspect her of treachery; the old Indian woman Nelema is tried as a witch, imprisoned, and sentenced to death; Hope's foster father sends her, against her will, to live with Governor Winthrop and his wife in an effort to tame her rebellious high spirits; and the archvillain of the novel, the Catholic Sir Philip Gardiner, has seduced a young orphan girl who is now his captive mistress, forced to travel with him, disguised as his valet, and endure his cruelties.

The women can begin to dismantle this male hegemony, Sedgwick implies, if they are both strong enough to defy the men and intelligent enough to succeed in reeducating them. Hope Leslie defies the Puritan establishment of Boston by engineering the escapes of both Nelema and Magawisca from prison and by subsequently retaining her loyalty to the two Indian women. Magawisca helps to reeducate Hope's foster brother, Everell, by giving him her version of the events of the Pequod War, during which she was captured and her own older brother was killed. Everell's understanding of the war changes radically because he is hearing the story from an Indian, but especially because the teller is a woman:

> All the circumstances attending [the war] were still fresh in men's minds, and Everell had heard them detailed with the interest and particularity that belongs to recent adventures; but he had heard them in the language of the enemies and conquerors of the Pequods; and from Magawisca's lips they took a new form and hue; she seemed, to him, to embody nature's best gifts, and her feelings to be the inspiration of heaven. This version of an old story reminded him of the man and the lion in the fable. But here it was not merely changing sculptors to give the advantage to one or the other of the artist's subjects; but it was putting the chisel into the hands of truth, and giving it to whom it belonged. (53)

Magawisca and Hope, therefore, contribute to the weakening of the legalistic, masculine interpretations of both history and religion, feminizing them by tempering doctrine with humane "feelings." Hope's Christianity is expressed through her readiness to help the victims of injustice, even when they are Indians, and Magawisca's interpretation of recent history demonstrates to Everell (and to the reader) that political and social power are determined not by "superior natural force" but only by "adventitious circumstances" (54).

Magawisca's life with the white Fletcher family is educational for her, as well. Everell teaches her to read and introduces her to his favorite writers, including Spenser. His teaching "had opened the book of knowledge to her—had given subjects to her contemplative mind, beyond the mere perceptions of her senses; had in some measure dissipated the clouds of ignorance that hung over the forest-child" (263). She also learns that not all whites despise her because she is Indian; the children of the family, especially Everell and Hope, accept her as a friend and an equal. Sedgwick is very careful, however, to make it clear that Magawisca is an extraordinary young woman whose qualities distinguish her from other Indians and mark her, much as Child's young Charles Hobomok Conant is marked, as an especially good candidate for assimilation into the white community (via the white family). As the daughter of an important chief, she demonstrates a combination of dignity, aloofness, and modesty that "expressed a consciousness of high birth" (23). Her physical appearance is also an advantage: "Her face, although marked by the peculiarities of her race, was beautiful even to an European eye" (23). She thrives among the Fletchers, whose civilized, stable home Sedgwick obviously sees as a far more appropriate place for the nurturing of Magawisca's mind and character than the wigwams and temporary camps of her father's wandering, illiterate people.

Magawisca would clearly like to stay with the Fletchers, but she is torn between her new affection for them and her old loyalty to her father, Mononotto, who has sworn to take revenge on the whites for the death of his son. Mononotto forces Magawisca to make a decision when he attacks the Fletcher home, killing Mrs. Fletcher and her infant and taking Everell and Faith Leslie captive. Although Magawisca subsequently helps Everell to escape, sacrificing one of her arms in the process, she refuses to flee with him, choosing instead to remain with her father, as vengeful and cruel as he is. For Sedgwick, it is this act of filial piety that dooms Magawisca and separates her forever from the white women and children who are her intellectual peers and natural allies. Having made her choice, Magawisca becomes

the constant companion of her father; susceptible and contemplative, she soon imbibed his melancholy, and became as obedient to the im-

> pulse of his spirit, as the most faithful are to the fancied intimations
> of the Divinity. She was the priestess of the oracle. Her tenderness
> for Everell, and her grateful recollections of his lovely mother, she
> determined to sacrifice on the altar of national duty. (194–95)

In stifling her own ambitions and best natural instincts, yielding
instead to the demands of a possessive father, Magawisca recapitu-
lates the experience of the most oppressed of the Puritan women.[16]
Because she chooses self-sacrifice over rebellion against patriarchal
authority, she can play no further part in the narrative of American
progress. She fades into the wilderness with her father, and "that
which remains untold of their story, is lost in the deep, voiceless
obscurity of those unknown regions" (339).

Hope Leslie and Everell Fletcher offer Magawisca the chance to
join them in constituting a new, vital American family that is not
defined by race; they also offer her models of a new kind of Christianity that is not defined by an exclusionary dogma. The freedom
available to all three of the young people has been made possible by
the sacrifices of their mothers, not their fathers; the fathers, in fact,
embody the narrow repressiveness that stands in the way of the
children's freedom. At one point, Hope and Magawisca meet over
the graves of their mothers, both of whose lives were spent in various
kinds of bondage to dominating males. " 'Think ye not,' " Magawisca says to Hope, " 'that the Great Spirit looks down on these
sacred spots, where the good and the peaceful rest, with an equal
eye; think ye not their children are His children, whether they are
gathered in yonder temple where your people worship, or bow to
Him beneath the green boughs of the forest?' " (189). The potential
is clearly there in Magawisca to become part of the new, feminized
realignments of family and faith in America. She chooses, however,
to remain loyal to her domineering Indian father, and so condemns
herself to a wandering obscurity and permanent separation from
white civilization and all that it has to offer.

At the moment Magawisca resumes her life with her father, she
also begins to resume the characteristics of the generic Indian of this
novel, including the characteristic that Sedgwick sees as the greatest

obstacle to Indian-white harmony: the Indian's instinct for revenge. In affirming her loyalty to Mononotto, the "ruthless, vengeful savage" (72), Magawisca must also affirm the commitment to revenge that, according to Sedgwick, is the hallmark of the true savage: " '[T]he law of vengeance is written on our hearts—you say you have a written rule of forgiveness—it may be better—if ye would be guided by it—it is not for us—the Indian and the white man can no more mingle, and become one, than day and night' " (330). The new, liberal version of Christianity represented by Hope and Everell—the prototype of Unitarianism—allows for, and even fosters, a spirit of tolerance and forgiveness; the Indian's religion, on the other hand, as close as it is to enlightened Christianity in most respects, does not allow for the forgiveness of one's enemies. The law of vengeance, according to Magawisca, is written on the Indian's heart.[17]

When Magawisca is tried for treachery by the Puritan magistrates, one of those present at the trial is John Eliot, the historical "Apostle Eliot" who devoted his ministry in New England to preaching to the Indians and translating the Bible into their language. Sedgwick's portrait of Eliot almost beatifies him: "an expression of love, compassion, and benevolence, seemed like the seal of his Creator affixed to declare him a minister of mercy to His creatures" (282). The appearance of this compassionate missionary as a character (the favorite, clearly, of *both* his creators) helps to point up the ignorance and bigotry of those other Puritans in the novel who continue to hold to "the notion that the Indians were the children of the devil" (286). Eliot's appearance is largely irrelevant to the plot, but so relevant to Sedgwick's thesis in the book that she provides a reinforcing footnote:

> We cannot pass the hallowed name of Eliot, without pausing earnestly to beseech our youthful readers to study his history, in which they will find exemplified, from youth to extreme old age, the divine precepts of his master. . . . His name has been appropriately given to a flourishing missionary station, where the principle on which he at all times insisted is acted upon, viz: "that the Indians must be civilized, as well as, if not in order to their being christianized." This principle

quality of the racist's Indian since at least the days of Cotton Mather. Sedgwick's Indians, that is, are still essentially the Puritan historians' Indians, and her model missionary is one who insisted that Indians could be saved only if they ceased to look, act, think, and talk like Indians.

Both Sedgwick and Child, therefore, for all their efforts to dismantle the racist stereotypes imposed on the Indians by the colonial historians, manage only to tinker with them. Their new versions of colonial history may successfully revise the Puritans' image of women as passive and inferior beings who have been relegated to the sidelines of history because that is their predestined place, but the changes they are willing to make in the images of Indians are, finally, only cosmetic. On the subject of Indians, in other words, the Puritan fathers will not be sent packing. In their rereading of history from the perspective of the 1820s, Child and Sedgwick declare that white American women are free to determine their own futures, while simultaneously concluding that the Indians, the companions of white women in the struggle against white patriarchal oppression, seem doomed to disappear into "deep voiceless obscurity," as they have already disappeared from the territory of New England, unless they can be persuaded to accept full assimilation into white culture. Although it might have been reasonable, even admirable, for the Indians to resist submission as long as white culture was controlled by Puritan males, continued resistance makes no sense now that the culture has become enlightened through its feminization. To put it another way, Child and Sedgwick end up only confirming the Puritan idea that the Indians are predestined to become extinct, since the only way they can be saved is to imitate the white women, and stop being Indians.

In *The Scarlet Letter*, Hawthorne also examines the place of women in Puritan America, this time from the perspective of midcentury; like Child and Sedgwick, he associates his female protagonist with the Indians (although in less direct ways), and reassesses the Puritan attitudes toward both women and Indians in the light of their subsequent histories. But unlike Child and Sedgwick, Hawthorne does

> has no opposers in our age, and we cannot but hope, that the prese
> enlightened labours of the followers of Eliot, will be rewarded wi
> such success, as shall convert the faint-hearted, the cold, and the ske
> tical, into ardent promoters of missions to the Indian race. (352–53)

The "hallowed" name of Eliot provides a sanction for the idea tha
Sedgwick is urging in her fictional portraits of Magawisca and her
father: that only a benevolent, enlightened form of Christianity can
save the Indians from their own vengeful nature and allow them to
participate in the full benefits of white civilization.

In making this statement in *Hope Leslie*, Sedgwick enters the
debates on the "Indan question" on the side of the reformers and
assimilationists. Her Magawisca is lost to savagery not because she
is inherently incapable of being civilized (after all, she likes reading
Spenser) but only because there is not a concerted effort to save her
that is strong enough to defeat the atavistic pull of her filial and racial
loyalty. Sedgwick, that is, aligns herself with the party that must
have seemed to her, in 1827, the most generous and forward-looking
(and most apolitical) in its attitude toward the future of the Indians.
And yet, in defining her position, she offers as her model a seventeenth-century orthodox Puritan minister whose purpose in preaching to the Indians was, in his words, to persuade them "to turn from
their lewd and lazy life to the living God, and to come forth from
the dark dungeon of their lost and ruined condition," who taught
them that "sins of the flesh" would bring "fire and flame to torment
your souls and bodies in all eternity," who did not believe that Indian
women should be taught to write, and who imposed fines or punish-
ments on the women among his converts for exposing their breasts
and on both women and men for wearing their hair long or killing
lice between their teeth.[18] Furthermore, in setting Eliot against the
other Puritan men, Sedgwick ignores the complicating fact that Cotton Mather, the arch-Puritan and archpatriarch, was also a promoter
of missions to the Indians, praising John Eliot for his project of "rais-
ing a number of these hedious [*sic*] creatures unto the elevation of
our holy religion."[19] In addition, even Sedgwick's "whitest" Indian,
Magawisca, is instinctively drawn to the desire for revenge—that Ur-

not conclude that the Puritans were wrong in the case of women and essentially right in the case of the Indians. The inconsistencies in *Hobomok* and *Hope Leslie* are, as I have suggested, the result of the writers' wish to proclaim the advent of a new American culture that is as progressive and democratic as the Puritan culture was static and exclusionary, and their subsequent inability to find a place within it for the unreconstructed American Indian, even a generously imagined one. Their portraits of women are meant to demonstrate that the Puritans were wrong in insisting that women are subservient and intellectually inferior because that is their God-given nature; yet their portraits of Indians only confirm the Puritan idea that there is such a thing as an Indian nature that has destined all Indians to inferiority and exclusion. Hawthorne's attitudes toward the Puritans, on the other hand, are much more consistent because he does not share the two women novelists' need to establish a gulf between the darkness of the seventeenth century and the enlightenment of the nineteenth century. Where they urge the possibilities of continued reform, he is deeply distrustful of the basic premise on which they base their appeal to readers: the premise that the errors of a deterministic theology have been dispelled, finally, by the light of reason, and that the barriers to individual and social advancement have thereby been removed. In short, Hawthorne finds the zeal for reform, the effort to change the power structures of American society that have always marginalized both white women and Indians, thoroughly and even dangerously naive.

By the time Hawthorne began *The Scarlet Letter*, the intellectual ferment of the Unitarian movement that Child and Sedgwick had welcomed so enthusiastically and optimistically had lost its revolutionary edge. The orthodox Congregationalists of New England had by no means vacated the field, and the most radical secular offshoot of the movement, transcendentalism, had produced some writing that was excitingly new and provocative but that few people outside the intellectual circles of eastern Massachusetts had even noticed. It was also clear by 1850 that the effort to "save" the Indians by removing them to the West had only resulted in new Indian wars, new ways of dying for the Indians, and new reasons for white authorities to want to move them out of the way once again. Perhaps most important, Hawthorne had made his own personal experiment in utopianism, joining the Brook Farm community briefly in 1841, and had found that he was temperamentally unsuited to the communal life and to constant manual labor; as he reported to his fiancée, "Even my Custom House experience was not such a thralldom and weariness; my mind and heart were freer."[20] All of these developments must at least have contributed to Hawthorne's skepticism about the validity of reform movements in general and his distrust of the people who made reform their business.

Hawthorne's resistance to organized efforts at reform was strong enough to lead him to disavow even the antislavery movement of the 1850s. In his campaign biography of Franklin Pierce, written in 1852, Hawthorne defended Pierce's opposition to the Compromise of 1850 on the grounds that Pierce, as a true statesman, recognized both the divisiveness of the antislavery movement and its ultimate impotence:

> And if the work of anti-slavery agitation, which it is undeniable leaves most men who earnestly engage in it with only half a country in their affections,—if this work must be done, let others do it.
>
> . . . But there is still another view . . . [which] looks upon slavery as one of those evils which divine Providence does not leave to be remedied by human contrivances, but which, in its own good time, by some means impossible to be anticipated, but of the simplest and easiest operation, when all its uses shall have been fulfilled, it causes to vanish like a dream. There is no instance, in all history, of the human will and intellect having perfected any great moral reform by methods which it adapted to that end; but the progress of the world, at every step, leaves some evil or wrong on the path behind it, which the wisest of mankind, of their own set purpose, could never have found the way to rectify.[21]

Hawthorne's stance here could easily be attributed to the fact that in agreeing to write a campaign biography he committed himself to justifying Pierce's political record by whatever circuitous or casuistical reasoning he could contrive. His general antipathy to efforts at "great moral reform" might just as easily be seen as the result of his having witnessed the failure of a number of specific movements to bring about any significant change. However, a survey of Hawthorne's published writing suggests that he had less practical, more visceral reasons for declaring that social evils could be remedied only when Providence, "in its own good time," caused them to disappear, and not when well-intentioned individuals decided to start cleaning things up. That is, the view he expresses in the Pierce biography— that social change is dependent on divine rather than human will and must await its proper time—is completely in keeping with the radically conservative view of social organization and social change that is expressed consistently in his writing.[22]

Hawthorne never directly or specifically addresses the "Indian question" in his published writings, but the few references to Indians he makes outside his fiction indicate that he saw the question of their place in American society as an issue that Providence had, for all practical purposes, already settled. In his journal for 1837–1840, for example, he notes that "our Indian races having reared no monuments, like the Greeks, Romans, and Egyptians, when they have disappeared from the earth, their history will appear a fable, and they misty phantoms."[23] In this observation Hawthorne assumes only that the Indians *will* disappear in time; however, when he writes about Indians in *The Whole History of Grandfather's Chair*, his history book for children, his assumption seems to be that they are already as good as extinct. Among the early Puritans that the grandfather-narrator in that book describes to the children gathered about his chair is John Eliot, the only one among the early settlers, according to the grandfather, who did not believe that the Indians were an inferior race of beings. Because he loved them and wanted to "deliver" them from their ignorance, he translated the Bible into their language and "persuaded as many of them as he could to leave off their idle and wandering habits, and to build houses and cultivate the earth, as the English did." In the grandfather's version, Eliot fears that if he doesn't live to finish his work of translation, "then must the red man wander in the dark wilderness of heathenism forever." One of the listening children is more disturbed than heartened by the story. " 'But it is a grievous thing to me,' " the child says,

" 'that he should have tried so hard to translate the Bible, and now the language and the people are gone! The Indian Bible itself is almost the only relic of both.' " Significantly, the grandfather does not contest the boy's idea that the Indians have already vanished; he only counsels him to remember and learn from the heroism of Eliot's effort to save the Indians—fruitless though it was.[24]

This story of Eliot, therefore, while it emphasizes his unique compassion, also illustrates for the children the inability of the reformer, no matter how well-meaning he or she might be, to have any significant or lasting effect on the course of history. Eliot's two legacies are a "relic" (an unreadable book) and a moral for young people. But the story also illustrates a subtler point for the children: the Indians are absent from the America the children know because they refused to be translated into English themselves—to abandon their "wandering habits" and do as the English did. In the grandfather's comments on the Indians, this notion of *wandering* is crucial; he names their wandering habits as the reason for their separation from civilized society, and he uses the image of "wander[ing] in the dark wilderness" to signify their morally and spiritually lost condition. In the rest of *Grandfather's Chair*, which follows American history through the Revolution, the Indians are not discussed again, as if the Eliot vignette had been sufficient to account for their presence in the past and their absence from the present. (When one of the children asks about King Philip's War, the grandfather says he does not have time to talk about it: " 'You must be content with knowing that it was the bloodiest war that the Indians had ever waged against the white men; and that, at its close, the English set King Philip's head upon a pole' " [58].)

The brief appearance of the Indians in this history for children is worth our attention, because Hawthorne presents here, in a simplified form, an idea that figures in the rest of his writing in more complex ways, the idea that all those who wander—who separate themselves from the communal sources of social, political, and moral stability, no matter how repressive those might seem to be—endanger their lives as well as their souls.[25] All of Hawthorne's wanderers face the choice between submission to the requirements of the stablizing community and moral disintegration. Or, to put it in other terms, they face the choice between civilization and extinction.

Hawthorne could hold up John Eliot as a model for children, even though he was a reformer, because Eliot stayed firmly within his Puritan community and worked to draw the others in, to turn the wandering outsiders into stable insiders. (The assumption is, of course, that those who build and cultivate are necessarily part of a stable social system, and that those who hunt or migrate are not.) His attitude toward reformers who deliberately place themselves outside the stable community, however, is very different, particularly when the reformer is a woman. In an essay on Anne Hutchinson that was first published in the *Salem Gazette* in 1830,[26] Hawthorne speaks of the hysteria that Mrs. Hutchinson aroused in her followers, especially the women, when she contested the moral and spiritual authority of the Puritan magistrates to dictate which forms of worship were permissible for the people of Massachusetts. Recreating the scene in which Mrs. Hutchinson defended herself before the magistrates, Hawthorne describes the women who listen to her as "shuddering and weeping," the young men as "fiery and impatient," all raised to a passionate pitch by the seditious eloquence of Mrs. Hutchinson's attack on the authorities in whom they had placed their trust: "Therefore their hearts are turning from those whom they had chosen to lead them to heaven; and they feel like children who have been enticed far from home, and see the features of their guides change all at once, assuming a fiendish shape in some frightful solitude."[27] This rather startling image of the listeners as vulnerable, betrayed children—emotional Hansels and Gretels confronting the witch—dramatizes (in its overdetermined way) a response to the self-proclaimed reformer, the nonconforming individual, that Hawthorne never really moved beyond. The image suggests that, for Hawthorne, what matters is not the specific content of Mrs. Hutchinson's speech, or whether her position is more or less reasonable than that of the magistrates; what matters is only that in attacking the sources of communal authority and stability, she creates panic in the community and betrays the "children" who rely on the community's protection and care.

Mrs. Hutchinson, whom Hawthorne calls a "reformer in religion," urged a religious freedom that was "wholly inconsistent with public safety" because it threatened to destroy the precarious unity of the young colony, leaving its citizens to wander, like lost and frightened children, with no moral and spiritual guides. Her ultimate fate, Hawthorne suggests, gives an ironic symmetry to the story of her life: she and a small band of her followers were attacked by Indians in the forest, "in the deep midnight"; the only person spared in the attack was "an infant daughter, the sole survivor amid the terrible destruction of her mother's household, [who] was bred in a barbarous faith, and never learned the way to the Christian's heaven." Because she would not submit to (masculine) authority and accept the compact by which the community preserved its unity, no matter how flawed the compact, Mrs. Hutchinson cast herself into the hands of "the savage foe" who lurked outside the community. And, significantly, the fate of her daughter translated into literal fact the metaphor of the child who suddenly finds herself in the hands of fiends.

Hawthorne had begun the essay by specifying for his readers the moral they might take away from the story of Mrs. Hutchinson. Women, he points out, are beginning to assert their "feminine ambition" by writing and publishing in such alarming numbers that the whole field of American literature seems on the verge of becoming monopolized by "ink-stained Amazons." Not only do women writers "add a girlish feebleness to the tottering infancy of our literature," they also risk alienating themselves forever from the rest of the "domestic race" of white American women once they take up the pen and thereby cross "the strong division lines of Nature." Therefore, "woman, when she feels the impulse of genius like a command of Heaven within her, should be aware that she is relinquishing a part of the loveliness of her sex, and obey the inward voice with sorrowing reluctance, like the Arabian maid who bewailed the gift of prophecy." Once this seemingly straightforward moral is attached to the story of Mrs. Hutchinson and her fate, its implications are deepened: the woman who sets herself in opposition to the male guardians of public safety and morality, whether by deliberately fostering a heresy or by expressing even safe opinions in print, crosses not only the natural line that divides male from female, but also the boundary that defines the limits of civilization.

Hawthorne returns to this thesis in his 1836 essay "The Duston Family."[28] The essay recounts the story of Hannah Duston, a Massachusetts mother of eight, who was captured by Indians (in 1698) and then effected an extraordinary escape: while her captors were sleeping, Mrs. Duston and another female captive, whom Mrs. Duston persuaded to join her, stole their tomahawks and killed ten of the twelve Indians, including six children. The original version of the Duston story appeared among the captivity narratives that Cotton Mather cited in his *Magnalia Christi Americana* as examples of the special providence of God in giving white Christians some notable victories over the devilish savages. Hawthorne, however, significantly revises Mather's version, not only by toning down its theological implications but, more important, by reversing its typological meaning, making Hannah Duston the villain of the story rather than its heroine.

Hawthorne describes Mrs. Duston after her killing of the Indians in language that suggests just how intense was his own emotional reaction to Mather's version. In Hawthorne's retelling, she becomes a "raging tigress," a "bloody old hag," whose story ought to have ended differently. It would have been better, Hawthorne says, if she had drowned in the river or sunk in the swamp,

> or . . . had gone astray and been starved to death in the forest, and nothing ever seen of her again, save her skeleton, with the ten scalps twisted round it for a girdle! But, on the contrary, she and her companions came safe home, and received the bounty on the dead Indians, besides liberal presents from private gentlemen, and fifty pounds from the Governor of Maryland.

These maledictions directed at Mrs. Duston come as a surprise to the reader largely because they are so inconsistent with the tone and direction of the earlier parts of the narrative. Mrs. Duston is at first referred to only as "the good woman," while the descriptions of the Indians are consistently Matheresque: they are the "raging savages," the "bloodthirsty foe," the "bloody Indians," even the "red devils," terrifying their victims with their "horrible visages . . . besmeared with blood." Yet by the end of the essay Mrs. Duston and the Indians have changed places: she is the one who is "raging" and "bloody" while the Indians have become a "copper-colored" version of what the Dustons once were, a peacefully sleeping family.

Although Hawthorne does not explain *how* the good woman becomes a savage (hence the reader's surprise), the essay does at least suggest that the transformation begins at the moment Mrs. Duston is forced to "follow the Indians into the dark gloom of the forest, hardly venturing to throw a parting glance at the blazing cottage, where she had dwelt happily with her husband, and had borne him eight children. . . . " When Mrs. Duston is removed from her domestic place and separated from her husband and children, she is simultaneously removed from all the constraints that made her the good woman. Forced to exchange the cottage for the dark forest, she rapidly ceases to be "woman" (since "woman" does not, *by definition*, kill children, even Indian ones) and becomes "hag" or witch, capable of out-Indianing the Indians: they killed one of her children, but she kills six of theirs. Their savagery pales before hers.[29]

The fates of some of Hawthorne's fictional women strongly recall these paradigmatic stories of Anne Hutchinson and Hannah Duston. In "The Gentle Boy," for example, the Quaker woman Catherine allows her religious "fanaticism" to draw her away from her child; the abandoned boy is taken in by a Puritan family, but they cannot protect him from the abuse of other children, who despise him because he is a Quaker. While her child suffers and declines, Catherine continues to "wander on a mistaken errand, neglectful of the holiest trust which can be committed to woman."[30] She leaves the domestic place to wander, physically and intellectually, and the ultimate result is the death of her child.

The most complex and interesting use Hawthorne makes of the Hutchinson-Duston pattern, however, is in *The Scarlet Letter*, and there he once again associates the female wanderer, the woman outside domesticity and community, with the Indians, and once again he sees her errantry as posing a threat to the life of her child. Hester Prynne differs somewhat from the other women in that she is capable of constructing her own metaphoric reading of her experience, consciously recognizing "the moral wilderness in which she had so long been wandering" (201). She also recognizes that the literal wilderness is a seductive place "where the wildness of her nature might assimilate itself with a people whose customs and life were alien from the law that had condemned her" (104). Mentally, Hester is an inhabitant of "desert places, where she roamed as freely as the wild Indian in his woods" (217). She is apparently not in any real danger of being literally captured or killed by Indians, as Mrs. Hutchinson and Mrs. Duston were, but she does put herself in the grave danger of moral dissolution by setting herself permanently outside the reach of those societal and ideological restraints that separate the American (white) woman from the savage.[31]

Of those restraints, the one that troubles Hester most deeply is the requirement that women must claim for themselves less freedom, of all kinds, than men do. She knows that "the whole race of womanhood" is held in subservience to men, denied their chance to occupy "a fair and suitable position." Yet she also knows that any attempt to change this imbalance would be "a hopeless task"; she would have to tear down "the whole system of society" to begin with, and then she would have to change "the very nature of the opposite sex" (184). Furthermore (as the narrator of the novel knows but Hester could not), in even contemplating these "preliminary reforms," Hester is on the verge of becoming another Ann Hutchinson or Hannah Duston—another woman who abandons her womanhood and gives herself to savagism, destroying a child in the process:

> Thus, Hester Prynne, whose heart had lost its regular and healthy throb, wandered without a clew in the dark labyrinth of mind; now turned aside by an insurmountable precipice; now starting back from a deep chasm. There was wild and ghastly scenery all around her, and a home and comfort nowhere. At times, a fearful doubt strove to possess her soul, whether it were not better to send Pearl at once to heaven, and go herself to such futurity as Eternal Justice should provide. (184)

Hester is saved from complete abandonment to the wild world only by the strength of her instinctive maternal attachment to Pearl, whose own womanhood she must nurture. Without Pearl to hold her back, Hawthorne says, Hester might have "come down to us in history, hand in hand with Ann [sic] Hutchinson" (183); she might, that is, have become another example of the waste of American womanhood in a futile effort to rid the world of one kind of injustice. Softened by her maternal devotion and by her suffering, Hester is finally brought to give up her dangerous ideas about reform and accept the position Hawthorne had taken in the Pierce biography: the changes that would free women (like those that would free slaves) will be brought about by something other than directed human will, and only in God's good time.[32] Hester spends her last days explaining to other women "her firm belief, that, at some brighter period, when the world should have grown ripe for it, in Heaven's own time, a new truth would be revealed, in order to establish the whole relation of man and woman on a surer ground of mutual happiness" (275).[33]

Hester saves herself, therefore, by ceasing to wander "like the wild Indian in his woods" and choosing assimilation into the Puritan patriarchy, as oppressive as it is. Hawthorne implies that the wisdom of her choice can be confirmed by considering the gains women have made over two hundred years, just by accepting their place and patiently waiting: they are no longer pilloried and branded for adultery or burned at the stake as witches. And because women have been content to accept their domestic place, nature has gradually gentled their condition: the "delicate, evanescent, and indescribable grace" (81) that characterizes nineteenth-century women is a far cry from the coarseness of their female ancestors, fed on English beef and ale, whose appropriate representative was "the man-like Elizabeth" (78). By the same token, the Indians, who persisted in their wandering, refusing to show any "reverence" for "the clerical band, the judicial robe, the pillory, the gallows, the fireside, or the church" (217), are now virtually absent from New England. Hester chose submission and assimilation, and the "race" of American womanhood has flourished; the Indians refused assimilation, and their race is, in Hawthorne's view, well on its way to a predictable extinction.

The moment of Hester's greatest temptation, the moment when she almost succumbs to the seductive illusion of moral freedom, occurs during her meeting with Dimmesdale in the forest. The setting itself encourages Hester and Dimmesdale in their reckless decision to leave Boston and find their freedom elsewhere: "Such was the sympathy of Nature—that wild, heathen Nature of the forest, never subjugated by human law, nor illumined by higher truth—with the bliss of these two spirits!" (220). Hester announces her freedom in this scene, first by removing her cap and literally (as well as metaphorically) letting down her hair, and then by throwing the scarlet letter, the mark of her carnal sin, into the woods. She urges Dimmesdale to consider the possibilities open to them; instead of resuming their lives in Boston, they could go further into the wilderness, where "some few miles hence, the yellow leaves will show no vestige of the white man's tread" (214). Hawthorne, however, makes it clear that the episode in the forest is only a kind of pathetic interlude, a moment of illusory freedom before the prison doors close again. To understand *why* the escape plan has no possible chance of success from the beginning, we need to notice that in the scene, Dimmesdale is waylaid by Hester as he is returning from a special errand: he has been to visit the Apostle Eliot "among his Indian converts" (200). Hester is wrong, therefore, in assuming that as long as she is in the woods beyond the town, the scarlet letter has no relevance; the Apostle Eliot is also in the woods, telling the Indians that lust is a deadly sin and, most significantly, that it is morally wrong for women to let their hair down. Appropriately, therefore, Pearl returns the scarlet letter to Hester, and Hester acknowledges that "the forest cannot hide it!" (227). As a white woman, and especially as a white mother, Hester cannot simply discard the restraints that separate her from the savages (including the restraints that hold her hair in place) without destroying her whole identity, and perhaps her life. The presence of Eliot, just a bit deeper in the woods, pursuing his mission of civilizing and christianizing the Indians by lecturing to them on lust and tying up their hair, is a reminder that the sine qua non of civilization is repression: the abridging of the freedoms of savage life. And the fact that his effort to save the wild Indians of the woods is doomed to failure, as the nineteenth-century reader would know, is a reminder that savagery and civilization cannot long coexist, in the individual or in America.

The alternative route of escape for Hester and Dimmesdale is the sea; the physical differences between forest and sea, however, count for very little in the moral scheme of Hawthorne's romance. Both are savage and unrestrained places, outside the defining and protecting limits of the patriarchal community, and equally threatening to any woman who might venture beyond those limits. Like the forest, the sea is subject to "hardly any attempts at regulation by human law" (247). Furthermore, the sea is the province of male wanderers who are the marine equivalent of the Indians of the forest. In the final scenes of the novel, when Hester comes to the Election Day festivities assuming that in a few hours she, Pearl, and Dimmesdale will take ship together and leave Boston for good, she finds both Indians and sailors among the assembled crowd. The appearance of the Indians in their holiday finery is arresting, but "wild as were these painted barbarians, [they] were [not] the wildest feature of the scene. This distinction could more justly be claimed by some mariners,—a part of the crew of the vessel from the Spanish Main" (247). These sailors are "the swarthy-cheeked wild men of the ocean, as the Indians were of the land" (258).

The very color of the "sun-blackened" sailors in this scene links them with the dark-skinned Indians in what is apparently for Hawthorne a sinister opposition to the whiteness of Puritan Boston, since the dark physiognomies are an index of the moral nature of both the sailors and the Indians: the eyes of the sailors have an "animal ferocity" (247), and the Indians have "snake-like black eyes" (259). The two groups of wild men are both drawn to Hester's scarlet letter, fastening their animal eyes on her breast with looks that clearly convey a sexual threat. The scene therefore constitutes a daylight version of those gatherings in the midnight forest that Mistress Hibbins, the witch, cackles about with such delight: gatherings where the Black Man presides and where one might see an "Indian powwow or a Lapland wizard changing hands with us!" (255). Mistress Hibbins knows (as does Hawthorne) that all Hester has to do is give her hand to an Indian or a sailor, and she will belong to the Black Man.

The sailors and Indians are further linked by their connection with Roger Chillingworth—whose own complexion has darkened from dusky to black as he has pursued his campaign of revenge against Dimmesdale. Chillingworth enters the novel in the company of an Indian, one of his captors, who has brought him to Boston to be redeemed. From her place on the scaffold Hester sees the Indian, and then sees that "by the Indian's side, and evidently sustaining a relationship with him, stood a white man, clad in a strange disarray of civilized and savage costume" (87). Chillingworth has apparently learned two things during his Indian captivity, both of which he will put to use in his attachment to Dimmesdale: the uses of herbal medicine, and the pleasures of revenge. In the final scene, Chillingworth once again enters the marketplace, the site of the scaffold, this time "in close and familiar talk" with the captain of the Spanish ship. By this point his original dalliance with revenge has become transformed into the obsession that gives his life satisfaction and meaning. Chillingworth's familiar relationship with the Indian and the sailor in these two scenes—the scenes that frame the novel—signifies his constant effort to maintain a liminal position, to live as a citizen of Boston without repressing the side of himself that allows him to be the companion of savages. The result is his steady moral and physical dissolution.

As Hester contemplates her escape by ship, the narrator pauses to wonder what is going on in the mind of this woman, "the people's victim and life-long bond-slave, as they fancied her" (242), who is now within hours of making her escape from seven years of bondage to a community that has allowed her practically no rights within it. Significantly, the length of her servitude is exactly the same as that of the indentured servants who have earned their passage to America by binding themselves to seven years of slave labor. Hester encounters one of these servants when she visits the home of Governor Bellingham: "a free-born Englishman, but now a seven years' slave. During that term he was to be the property of his master, and as much a commodity of bargain and sale as an ox, or a joint-stool" (126). The indentured servant, that is, submits himself to a humiliating bondage in order to earn his place in the community.

Hester is also released from her bondage after seven years, and leaves Boston for Europe. She returns, however, this time to resume the scarlet letter willingly and to spend the remainder of her sorrowful life as a counselor to the other women of Boston. If it seems that Hester has only exchanged an imposed bondage for a freely chosen one, then, Hawthorne reminds us, that exchange is the only one possible for any of the adult characters of the novel. The indentured servant, after all, must still submit to the stern and repressive laws of the community when he has earned his right to citizenship. Chillingworth leaves two years of Indian captivity only to become a captive to his own obsession with revenge, and Dimmesdale's one gesture toward escaping the limitations imposed on him as a Puritan minister makes him a slave to Chillingworth and to his own guilty self-loathing. Even the forest and the sea offer no real escape from the necessity of bondage, since, as Mistress Hibbins points out, "when the Black Man sees one of his own servants, signed and sealed, so shy of owning to the bond as is the Reverend Mr. Dimmesdale, he hath a way of ordering matters so that the mark shall be disclosed in open daylight to the eyes of all the world!" (255). For Hawthorne, then, the necessity of bondage and the consequent need to choose one's bondage carefully are components of all civilized life, but the need is especially great in America, where the tempting illusion of freedom in a new and open country can lead the unwary or the willful straight into the most dangerous kinds of captivity.

The moment when Chillingworth arrives in Boston to be redeemed out of his Indian captivity is the same moment that marks the real beginning of Hester's guilty abasement to the will of the Puritan community. Chillingworth and Hester meet and talk in the prison-house, where he awaits his freedom and she awaits the beginning of her new life of public shame. His captivity in the forest ends, that is, as hers in Boston begins, and hers seems the more oppressive of the two: "The chain that bound her here was of iron links, and galling to her inmost soul, but never could be broken" (105). As I have already suggested, in her mental wandering, her solitary journeys through the moral wilderness of free thought, Hester comes to resemble Hawthorne's version of Hannah Duston, the woman whose brief life with Indians leads her to the savagery of child murder. However, Hester's life in Boston also resembles the story of another famous Puritan captive, Mary Rowlandson, who was captured by Indians in 1676 but survived to be redeemed and to offer her story as an example of the faithfulness of God in protecting those whom he has chosen.

Like Hester, Rowlandson was taken with her young daughter, and like Hester, she earned the forbearance of her captors through her womanly skill as a seamstress, sewing shirts and baby dresses for the Indians. Rowlandson describes the disorientation of the early days of her captivity in terms that recall Hester's reactions as she stands on the scaffold. Frequently, Rowlandson says, she would find herself sitting in an Indian wigwam and "musing on things past," and then she would "suddenly leap up and run out, as if I had been at home, forgetting where I was, and what my condition was: But when I was without, and saw nothing but Wilderness, and Woods, and a company of barbarous heathens, my mind quickly returned to me. . . ."[34] Hester too begins to remember her life before she came to Boston, and the memories are strong enough to make the present scene disappear momentarily from view, until suddenly "in place of these shifting scenes, came back the rude market-place of the Puritan settlement, with all the townspeople assembled and levelling their stern regards at Hester Prynne. . . . Yes!—these were her realities,— all else had vanished!" (86). Rowlandson's life among the Indians strengthens her faith in Calvinist theology by putting it through a severe test, as it strengthens her will to return to the safety, both spiritual and physical, of her family and her Puritan community. Hester's captivity by the Puritans, on the other hand, strengthens her desire to be as morally free as the Indians, and her will to take her own destiny—and that of other women—out of the hands of a Calvinist God or even a benign Providence. But according to the argument of *The Scarlet Letter*, both women are really wishing to exchange one captivity for another, and according to Hawthorne's view of history, the Puritan form of captivity was necessary in order to save future women from the fate of Mary Rowlandson, Hannah Duston, Ann Hutchinson, or Hester Prynne. The Puritan captivity confined women to the place they were meant by nature to occupy, at least until the new revelation, and it rid that place of the threat of savagery.

In this discussion of *The Scarlet Letter* I have argued that Hawthorne brings together in the novel a number of themes—the place of women, the uselessness of reform movements, the moral dangers to which reformers expose themselves, the disappearance of the Indians—that might seem at first glance only tangentially related to each other. However, this odd ganglion of themes is one that Hawthorne seemed to have no wish to disentangle, since he returns to it in two more books, *The Blithedale Romance* and the unfinished *Septimius Felton*. *Blithedale* is about a utopian community that succumbs (as one could argue that the utopian ambitions of Puritan Boston do in *The Scarlet Letter*) to the divisive tensions caused by sexual desire and sexual jealousy. At one point in the novel four members of the community meet in the woods at "Eliot's pulpit," the rock where local legend has determined that John Eliot delivered his sermons to the Indians. The conversation turns to the role of women; the most ardent and passionate of the female members of the community, Zenobia, announces her belief that "the pen is not for woman. Her power is too natural and immediate. It is with the living voice alone that she can compel the world to recognize the light of her intellect and the depth of her heart!"[35] In taking this stand Zenobia is in agreement not only with Hawthorne, who expressed his wish (in 1852, the year he published *Blithedale*) that all women would be forbidden to write "on pain of having their faces deeply scarified with an oyster-shell,"[36] but also with John Eliot, who was willing to teach Indian women to read but not to write. The shade of Eliot is present in more ways than this, however, since the very absence of Indians from the place that Blithedale now occupies is evidence of the failure of Eliot's effort to save them; his pulpit *ought* to be a reminder to the gathered group of reformers that their own brand of utopianism is as doomed as Eliot's was. Even Zenobia's impassioned speech about the intellect and heart of woman is immediately undercut by one of the males present, Hollingsworth, who declares that woman's place is at man's side, her duty only to sympathize with him and believe in him. Significantly, Zenobia does not contest Hollingsworth; her argument is therefore self-canceling, since her "living voice" has had no more power to change her audience than Eliot's did when he stood in his pulpit.[37]

In *Septimius Felton*, which Hawthorne began in 1861 and fiddled with for years without ever finishing, his treatment of this knot of themes is less subtle than it is in the other two novels, and his attitude toward both reformers and Indians is more cynical. His protagonist, Septimius, is of mixed blood, descended on one side from a long line of "chiefs, and sachems, and Pow-wows."[38] He lives with his aunt Keziah, who is also of mixed blood, "as strange a mixture of an old Indian squaw and herb doctress, with the crabbed old maid, and a mingling of the witch-aspect running through all, as could be imagined" (304–5). Septimius has the most radically utopian desire of any of Hawthorne's characters: he wants the secret of immortality. Through Keziah, he comes into possession of an elixir that was invented by his and Keziah's ancestor, an old Indian sachem, and that once had the power to confer immortality. The sachem, a reformer in his own way, made use of his recipe to prolong his life long beyond its natural limits; however, he eventually grew tired of living, having "learned to despair of ever making the red race much better than they now were" (318). Therefore, he removed the one essential ingredient from the elixir before he passed it on, replacing it with "firewater" and thus giving it, from Keziah's point of view, "the only one thing that it wanted to make it perfect" (317). This little history of the elixir therefore encapsulates one version—presumably the version Hawthorne found most appropriate—of the history of the Indians in America: having resisted efforts to help them survive by making them better than they were, the Indians dwindled to a small remnant of useless and discontented half-breeds, given to the pleasures of "fire-water."

Septimius is not the only character in the novel with utopian fantasies; he forms an alliance at one point with a young woman named Sybil Dacy, who says that she too would like to be immortal, and she and Septimius discuss the ways they might spend their eternal life. Sybil toys with the idea of spending her time figuring out whether she can save women from all their troubles, but thinks that even with infinite time to work on the problem, she still might conclude that the only solution would be to kill all female children. Septimius's response to Sybil is to express his hope that " 'we shall be able to hush up this weary and perpetual wail of womankind on easier terms than that' " (406). Keziah, too, wishes her life were radically different; she is unhappy about having several half-identities and no single, complete one. Rather than wishing for immortality, therefore, which would only prolong her present unhappiness, she fantasizes about being reincarnated as a full-blooded Indian or, especially, as a real witch. From her broomstick, Keziah says, she would be able to look down on a witch's world and see it with a witch's eye: " 'There is an Indian; there a nigger; they all have equal rights and privileges at a witch-meeting' " (358).

Since Hawthorne did not finish this novel, we cannot know for certain how he meant for the reader finally to understand these statements. They are, however, consistent with the attitudes he expresses in *The Scarlet Letter* and other places, only more boldly stated here. For a woman to contemplate her status and her rights must eventually lead her to contemplate murdering female children. And to imagine a state of things in which Indians and blacks have "equal rights and privileges" is to take the broomstick view, to indulge in magical thinking—as unrealistic as witchcraft, as dangerous, and as madly anachronistic.

In his sketch of "The Old Manse," first published in 1846, Hawthorne takes the reader on a leisurely tour of the Manse, his new home, and its surroundings. Adjacent to the Manse is the site of an old Indian village, where relics are still to be found. Remembering what used to be there, Hawthorne recreates the scene in his mind: a quiet, peaceful village with "painted chiefs and warriors," squaws, and papooses. The serenity of the imagined scene leads him to wonder if "it is a joy or a pain, after such a momentary vision, to gaze around in the broad daylight of reality" at the relatively colorless, pedestrian activities and "homespun pantaloons" of the contemporary village of Concord that has replaced the Indian village. The question, however, is quickly overridden: "But this is nonsense. The old Manse is better than a thousand wigwams."[39]

This abruptly stated conclusion is also the one that is implicit in the novels by Child and Sedgwick, as far removed from Hawthorne as both women are in their vision of the Indians' place in America's past and future. Child and Sedgwick both see the saving of the remaining Indians—by moving them out of their wigwams and into the liberal, Protestant culture (the Manse) of white America—as part of the moral mission of the country. Their critiques of colonial culture contain the charge that the Puritan treatment of Indians was bigoted and morally indefensible, and their appeals to their audiences contain the implication that the national guilt that is the legacy of the earlier history can be eradicated, for good, by the new generation of enlightened Americans. In offering their appeals, both women present American history in terms of an incomplete family saga, in which the healthier, bolder (white) children of the family have flourished and matured, while the weaker, less adaptable (Indian) children have been either neglected or actively abused. For them, the moral challenge to the America of the 1820s is to rid itself of guilt by attempting to bring the lost children, gently and by degrees, into the "Manse" of white America.

Hawthorne also writes about history by writing about families; what is missing from his families, however, is not the weak Indian children but the strong white fathers. Anne Hutchinson is murdered and her daughter stolen by Indians because she puts herself beyond male protection (and reduces her husband to a pale adjunct); Hannah Duston becomes a savage, a killer of children, when she is removed from her husband's home; and Hester Prynne comes close to complete moral dissolution—close to joining the Indian savages—because Dimmesdale will not acknowledge his place as her husband and the father of her daughter. In all three cases, the children are at best threatened with death and at worst killed because of the absence or weakness of the male, the source of protection, discipline, and sometimes outright repression. Without their fathers, the white children, especially the girls, are vulnerable; they become the potential victims of every kind of savagery. Hawthorne's Puritans, then, are made to

appear prescient in their repressiveness and in their determination to
rid the American place of its savages. And *his* Puritans know that
guilt is both a fine agent of repression and a necessary part of personal
and national life. For Hawthorne, guilt is not the result of killing
savages but of imitating them. His old Manse, where the previous
occupant pored over his yellowed theological treatises and prepared
his sermons, is a small monument to New England Protestant guilt,
but certainly not because it has replaced an Indian village. The village
had to go to make the Manse possible, and one manse is, after all,
worth a thousand wigwams.

Sedgwick and Child are also far removed from Hawthorne in their
attitudes toward the place of the Indians in American literature. Their
Indians, stereotyped though they are, are still granted the status of
individualized characters, and their fates are the source of the strongest emotional appeals of the two novels. Assuming that both writers
expected their audiences to be made up largely of women, we can
also assume that both expected most of their female readers to be
receptive to their new, feminized versions of American history and
their portrayals of the Indians as *prospective* members of the recon-
stituted American family. This new audience, that is, should be
pleased to see the Indians freed from the monopoly of frontier fiction—the province of male writers—and offered a home with the
domestic novelists. Hawthorne's Indians, on the other hand, are only
generic symbols, not characters; they have no names and no separate
identities. When Hester reenters her old house at the end of *The
Scarlet Letter*, ceasing to wander like the wild Indian in his woods
and accepting her appropriate public identity, the Indians, and all
they represent, have no more function and are banished from the
novel. Whether Hawthorne had read *Hobomok* and *Hope Leslie* or
not, he still ended *The Scarlet Letter* with a message that might have
been addressed to the women who wrote them: if women writers
would reenter their own houses, where they belong, American literature might soon be rid of a lot of its wild Indians.

4 | *Points of Departure:*
Fuller, Thoreau,
and Parkman

IN THE SUMMER of 1843, Margaret Fuller set off for a tour of the region of the Great Lakes. Three years later, in 1846, Francis Parkman and Henry David Thoreau also set off on excursions; Parkman's trip took him west on the newly opened Oregon Trail into what is now eastern Wyoming, and Thoreau's took him north to Mt. Ktaadn in Maine. All three travelers were New Englanders, all starting out from the part of the United States that Margaret Fuller confidently described as "a chief mental focus of the New World," the place where "what is to be acted out in the country at large is most frequently indicated, as all the phenomena of the nervous system in the fantasies of the brain . . . ."[1] All three made their forays out of New England with their pencils firmly in hand, and all returned with the collections of notes they would turn into the published accounts of their travels. Fuller's notes resulted in *Summer on the Lakes* (1844), her first book, and Parkman's resulted in *The Oregon Trail* (1849), his first book. Thoreau's notes became an essay ("Ktaadn") for the *Union Magazine*. Thoreau subsequently made two more trips to Maine, in 1853 and 1857, both of which he also wrote about. The second account ("Chesuncook") was published in the *Atlantic Monthly*; the third ("The Allegash and East Branch") remained unpublished until William Ellery Channing put the three accounts together, after Thoreau's death, and published the collection under the title *The Maine Woods* (1864).

The travel accounts of all three writers are, to varying extents, records not only of their traveling but also of their preparation for writing larger, more ambitious works. Fuller's descriptions of life in the frontier settlements around the Great Lakes become increasingly focused on the status of frontier women, white and Indian, and many of the anecdotes she first records in *Summer on the Lakes* are repeated—having become examples used to support Fuller's argument for female equality—in *Woman in the Nineteenth Century*. That book, published in 1845, was a revised and expanded version of Fuller's article "The Great Lawsuit—Man *versus* Men; Woman *versus* Women" that had appeared in the *Dial* in July of 1843, while Fuller was in the middle of her tour of the lakes. She returned from the trip with new material to strengthen and extend the argument of the article—stories about the absurdity of frontier mothers who insist on preparing their daughters to inhabit drawing rooms rather than log cabins, and about the painful condition of Indian women, who "inherit submission" and learn to "accommodate themselves more or less to any posture."[2]

Thoreau's three Maine essays also seem notes for a larger work. He took the first trip to Maine at the end of his second summer at Walden, when he was working on *A Week on the Concord and Merrimack Rivers* and experimenting with life in the woods, and there is much about the "Ktaadn" essay that makes it seem an extension of the material he had been collecting back in Massachusetts, an effort to take his collecting deeper into the woods in search of purer and rarer specimens. In Maine, he says in "Ktaadn," "some hours only of travel . . . will carry the curious to the verge of a primitive forest, more interesting, perhaps, on all accounts, than they would reach by going a thousand miles westward."[3] The Maine trip gave him a literal wilderness experience on which he could draw in describing his "wild" life in the merely rural, countrified neighborhood of Concord.

The other two Maine trips, however, were taken after Thoreau had published both *Walden* and *A Week*, and although in his accounts of both these trips Thoreau seems to be deliberately collecting material and consciously writing proleptically, it is not clear exactly what kind of project he had in mind. He may have intended putting together the three Maine accounts and publishing them as a single book himself, but if so, he was prevented by the realization that his third and longest account, "The Allegash and East Branch," was, as he saw it, unprintable. As he wrote to James Russell Lowell in 1858, "The more fatal objection to printing my last Maine-wood experience, is that my Indian guide, whose words & deeds I report very faithfully,—and they are the most interesting part of the story,—knows how to read, and takes a newspaper, so that I could not face him again."[4] Still, he did write an account of the trip, and in that account and the previous one, "Chesuncook," Thoreau acknowledges that there is a specific purpose for all his observing and note-taking: if he was after primitive wilderness on his first trip, on these two trips he is after Indians, the primitive men. Early in "Chesuncook" he writes of watching the Indian guide, Joe Aitteon, repairing a canoe: "I narrowly watched his motions, and listened attentively to his observations, for we had employed an Indian mainly that I might have an opportunity to study his ways" (105). Four years later Thoreau again hired an Indian guide, this time the Joe Polis whose ability to read kept Thoreau from publishing his observations, and this time Thoreau was not content to study the ways of the Indian by covertly watching one. He makes his intentions known at the beginning of the essay: "I told [Polis] that in this voyage I would tell him all I knew, and he should tell me all he knew, to which he readily agreed" (186).

These two trips were made during the period (1847 to 1861) when Thoreau was steadily filling twelve notebooks—his "Indian Books"—with notes, anecdotes, and transcribed passages from his reading about Indians. Robert F. Sayre, who studied the twelve notebooks carefully, has argued that Thoreau probably had no plan to publish a book based on the information in his notebooks, at least not until he could supplement it with more experiences of personal contact with living Indians. We know that he refused to publish what he had written about Joe Polis, and, Sayre argues, "without [Polis] Thoreau would have to rely mainly on material in his Indian commonplace books, and it all came from other writers. That was not his kind of book." Sayre concludes that Thoreau continued to collect his information on Indians not necessarily with an eye to publication, but because his commonplace books "were stimulating and pleasurable to keep. They were a means of discovery, not only about Indians but about the natural history of America. Such discoveries, in turn, provoked him, while on his walks and travels, into fresh observations and a keener sense of the world, an Indian eye." Sayre's argument is appealing, but as even he admits, "Thoreau did not make long excursions like [his Maine trips] without thinking of books and essays."[5] Nor is there convincing evidence anywhere in his writing that Thoreau was reluctant to construct his own texts out of the discoveries he had made in other people's texts. It finally seems, in short, that on his Maine trips Thoreau *was* collecting material for an Indian book, or that at least he was collecting Indian material for *some* kind of book; even if he couldn't publish what he had written about Polis, he could use what he had learned from him.

Of the three travel accounts under consideration here, Francis Parkman's *Oregon Trail* is the one that was most obviously and most self-consciously undertaken as part of the writer's preparation for a different and more demanding book. Parkman had set himself an ambitious first project: to write a book about the conquest of Canada as a significant turning point in the history of North America, the point at which the American Indians suffered the series of defeats that was to force them into decline and, as Parkman saw it, into eventual extinction. In the course of his early researches for the book, Parkman became convinced that he could not write authoritatively about Indians without spending some time among them. As he wrote in an 1845 letter, his reading about Indians had led him to "one certain result—that their character will always remain more or less of a mystery to one who does not add practical observation to his closest studies. In fact, I am more than half resolved to devote a few months to visiting the distant tribes." By March of 1846 he had determined that his book would focus on the figure of the Ottawa chief Pontiac and that it would be useful to see what kind of reputation, if any, Pontiac still had among living Indians in the West. In a letter written that March, Parkman noted that Pontiac

> seems to be looked back upon as a hero, by the Indians—is it not possible that something might be gathered by personal inquiry among them? Such authority, to be sure, would be very apochryphal, but then one may retain the right of judging for himself, and as I propose to visit the northern and western tribes, I shall have good opportunity for such investigations.[6]

Later that spring Parkman made his visit, one that he described in the preface to *The Oregon Trail* as "undertaken on the writer's part with a view of studying the manners and character of Indians in their primitive state."[7] As his letter indicates, however, Parkman went on his trip prepared to grant authority only to his own *judgments* and to discount as apocryphal any testimony of the Indians that did not accord with them. He returned in the fall ready to proceed with his history book, *The Conspiracy of Pontiac and the Indian War After the Conquest of Canada* (published in 1851), apparently confident that he could now explain "the Indian race" to white readers.

Not surprisingly, all three writers prepared for their trips—and therefore for their narratives—by reading extensively in what others had written about their own encounters with Indians. (As Todorov notes, "Is not a travel narrative itself the point of departure, and not only the point of arrival, of a new voyage? Did not Columbus himself set sail because he had read Marco Polo's narrative?")[8] Fuller reports in *Summer on the Lakes* that the best book on Indians she read in preparation for her tour was George Catlin's, but that she also made her way through Schoolcraft's *Algic Researches* and the travel accounts of (at least) Murray, McKenney, Irving, and Mrs. Jameson. Thoreau does not say much about his preparatory reading in the essays of *The Maine Woods*, but we know from the references in *A Week* and from his journals that he was already collecting information about Indians when he made his first trip, and by the time of the second trip he had begun transcribing the hundreds of pages of material that went into the Indian notebooks. Parkman's decision to travel out West was taken in part because, according to him, he had read "almost all the works on the Indians, from Lafitau and the Jesuits down to the autobiography of Black Hawk," and found them inadequate; he needed to see for himself.[9]

In considering the similarities of circumstance in which these three writers made their trips and produced their narratives, we can see that for each the traveling itself was an essentially literary undertaking: the true point of departure in each case was a body of literature, the ultimate object of traveling was to revise the literature, and the projected audience consisted of those New England readers for whom "the Indian problem" was, already, primarily an intellectual and aesthetic issue. Each of the three trips originated in reading and eventuated in publishing, and each traveler evidently wrote throughout the trip, taking notes for a travel narrative that would be, at the same time, a sourcebook of information for a different and more ambitious literary project. Furthermore, each traveler/writer set out from literate, literary New England, the "brain" of the country in Margaret Fuller's metaphor, to study and report on a group of largely illiterate subjects who would never be able to read what was written about them. In fact, as Thoreau's concern about Joe Polis suggests, it was the traveler's knowledge of the illiteracy of the people written about that made it possible for the traveler to publish what he or she had written. And for each of these writers, the need to write something about the Indians was urgent: Fuller believed that "this race is fated to perish" (195); Thoreau was convinced that the Indians would be "soon exterminated" (133); and Parkman was equally sure that within a century the Indians would be "[swept] from the face of the earth" (141). Each writer's project, then, is to present the illiterate to the literate through a text, to make the Indians-as-subjects "readable" to a distanced, non-Indian audience, while at the same time maintaining the writer's credibility as a reliable witness of the Indians-as-objects. Each writer must, that is, find a way of interpreting the living Indians, who are (in the writer's view) illiterate, uncivilized, and moribund, so that they become available for preservation in a text that readers back home in the cities and towns of New England will find both "civilized" and credible.

To put it yet another way, the trick is to save the "savages" in the text, without letting their very savagery destroy the text.

On the question of who is best qualified to accomplish this important project of interpretation and preservation, the three writers appear to represent two diametrically opposed positions. Fuller and Thoreau agree that the only truly accurate interpretations of the Indians and the wilderness must come from outside, from observers (like themselves) who approach with a fresh eye and, especially, an educated poetic sensibility.[10] Fuller notes, for example, that those people who have spent all their lives among Indians "have been men better fitted to enjoy and adapt themselves to this life, than to observe and record it. The very faculties that made it so easy for them to live in the present moment, were likely to unfit them for keeping its chronicle" (200). She finds that even those travelers whose accounts seem most scrupulously accurate can actually distort their subjects by being *too* concerned with the literal; "We believe," she says, "the Indian cannot be looked at truly except by a poetic eye" (31). Thoreau's experiences in the Maine woods lead him to a similar conclusion. On the second trip, he watches his Indian guide kill and butcher a moose and turns away in disgust, consoling himself that he, Thoreau, understands the wilds better than do the wild men he has come to observe and learn from. The moose-killing, he says,

> suggested to me how base or coarse are the motives which commonly carry men into the wilderness.... For one that comes with a pencil to sketch or sing, a thousand come with an axe or rifle. What a coarse and imperfect use Indians and hunters make of nature! No wonder that their race is so soon exterminated. (133)

Thoreau has obviously come to the wilderness equipped with his own pencil, ready to *write* the axe- and rifle-wielders out of the way: "Is it the lumberman, then, who is the friend and lover of the pine, stands nearest to it, and understands its nature best?... No! no! it is the poet.... No, it is the poet, who loves them as his own shadow in the air, and lets them stand" (135).

Parkman might seem to stand at the opposite extreme from Fuller

and Thoreau, since he would banish all poets from *his* Indian territory. He sets out deliberately to reclaim the Indians from the poetic
writers and restore them to the responsible historians, specifically
offering his narrative as a corrective to the poets' pictures of the
Indians. His trip takes him, he says, hundreds of miles beyond "the
prairies of the poet and the novelist"; these prairies are to be found
on the edge of the frontier settlements, where both the landscape and
the Indians are tame and unthreatening and therefore, in Parkman's
view, not the genuine article (457). In writing about what lies beyond
the relatively tame frontier, Parkman explains in the preface to *The
Oregon Trail*, his only aim is to give readers a completely reliable
and unfanciful report of what is actually out there:

> In justifying [my] claim to accuracy on this point, it is hardly necessary
> to advert to the representations given by poets and novelists, which,
> for the most part, are mere creations of fancy. The Indian is certainly
> entitled to a high rank among savages, but his good qualities are not
> those of an Uncas or an Outalissi.[11] (34)

Thoreau goes to the forest-wilderness with only a pencil in hand;
Parkman goes to the prairie-wilderness with a pencil in one hand and
a rifle in the other, ready to use the former on the poets' Indians he
has read about and the latter on the real Indians he encounters:
"Trust not an Indian. Let your rifle be ever in your hand" (201). In
making clear his pronounced dislike of belletristic treatments of the
Indians, Parkman seems to have deliberately removed himself as far
as possible from writers like Fuller and Thoreau. The epigraph for
his book might easily have been "Trust not a poet."

However, as I will argue later in this chapter, Parkman's relentless
effort at demythologizing the Indians in *The Oregon Trail* can actually be seen, retrospectively, as a way of preparing himself, his
readers, and "his" Indians for the great project of *re*mythologizing
that he was to undertake in his next book, *The Conspiracy of Pontiac*.
In attempting to retrieve the Indians from the poets and restore them
to the historians, Parkman was in fact only rejecting one kind of
literary paradigm in favor of another that he saw as more stable.
From our point of view, then, we can see that the three writers finally

share a common perspective on the question of writing about Indians; for all three, it is only the fully reconstructed and mythologized Indian—one who lives nowhere in nineteenth-century America—who can be assimilated into the civilized American text.

Margaret Fuller's instincts as a traveler as well as a writer were those of the liberal reformer, one whose relentless (and ironically ahistorical) optimism kept her convinced that whatever future an individual or a country might imagine could be eventually attained. The future of the United States, as she defines it in *Woman in the Nineteenth Century*, has a special significance for all of human history: "This country is as surely destined to elucidate a great moral law, as Europe was to promote the mental culture of Man."[12] Since the great law to which she alludes is the law that all men are created equal—morally and intellectually as well as politically—Fuller can go on to argue that all forms of oppression in America, whether enforced by law or by custom, will eventually be eliminated as the country moves inexorably toward the fulfillment of its destiny: "That which has been conceived in the intelligence cannot fail, sooner or later, to be acted out" (26).

Her vision of the mature America of the future, the one that has achieved its destiny, is of a fully harmonized society:

> When the same community of life and consciousness of mind begin among men, humanity will have, positively and finally, subjugated its brute elements and Titanic childhood; criticism will have perished; arbitrary limits and ignorant censure be impossible; all will have entered upon the liberty of law, and the harmony of common growth. (118)

Although Fuller is chiefly concerned in *Woman in the Nineteenth Century* with the status of (white) women, she acknowledges that there are other, more widely visible forms of oppression that are condoned in America, if nowhere else: "I need not speak of what has been done towards the Red Man, the Black Man. Those deeds are the scoff of the world" (25). Fuller goes on to say more about "the Black Man" in America, specifically linking the movement for women's rights to the antislavery movement and predicting that they will eventually result in the emancipation of both women and blacks in the new America. Of "the Red Man," however, she has no more to say here; she had already confronted the question of the Indians' participation in the society to come in *Summer on the Lakes,* and had concluded that their political destiny was not to be equality within a free society but inevitable removal from it. If imagination urged her to look forward to envision the destiny of women and blacks in America, it could only urge her to look backward to find models that would allow her to articulate her perception of the Indians' destiny.[13]

Fuller may have gone to the frontier intending to look about her with a poet's eye, but it is primarily with the eye of the critical reader of poetry that she actually sees. The frontier of *Summer on the Lakes* is, for her, essentially the mass of raw material out of which the new American culture and, more important, the new American literature are to be shaped. The immediate prospect, however, is daunting: the white settlers, she finds, are acquisitive and calculating; the Indians are dirty and frequently drunk, and they smell bad; the forests are being destroyed as fast as the settlers can cut them down. To see the potential for anything culturally or aesthetically promising in this anarchical prospect requires, for Fuller, a tremendous act of faith, which she acknowledges near the beginning of her narrative:

> I come to the west prepared for the distaste I may experience at its mushroom growth. I know that where 'go ahead' is the only motto, the village cannot grow into the gentle proportions that successive lives, and the gradations of experience involuntarily give. . . . I have come prepared to see all this, to dislike it, but not with stupid narrowness to distrust or defame. On the contrary, while I will not be so obliging as to confound ugliness with beauty, discord with harmony, and laud and be contented with all I meet, when it conflicts with my best desires and tastes, I trust by reverent faith to woo the mighty meaning of the scene, perhaps to foresee the law by which a new order, a new poetry is to be evoked from this chaos. . . . (28)

Where a Walt Whitman might have exulted in the sheer bustle and energy of the frontier settlements, Fuller recoils from them; where a Whitman might have looked straight on and happily catalogued the details of all he saw, declaring that his disorderly catalogues *are* the new American poetry, Fuller is more inclined to look away from the scene and scan her mental shelf of classics for appropriate metaphors that will dignify the American chaos. To manage her impressions, she determines that she must "call up the apparitions of future kings from the strange ingredients of the witch's caldron" (28) without examining the distasteful ingredients of the witch's brew too closely; rather than cataloging specific details, she will instead register and record "the poetic impression of the country at large" (67).

Fuller's prescriptions for the "new poetry" to be evoked from the American scene seem to come, somewhat paradoxically, from her reading of classical sources. Her American poet will follow Plato in avoiding all forms of imitation, as he will follow Aristotle in using his poetry as a means of locating the universal and the timeless within the particular scenes he observes. (In this regard, Fuller is perhaps one of the few writers to whom the term *American Renaissance* has a fully meaningful relevance.) In her essay on the current state of American literature, published in 1846, she notes that American writers are still imitating the English and that there is, therefore, not yet a body of literature that can be called genuinely American: "Books which imitate or represent the thoughts and life of Europe do not constitute an American literature. Before such can exist, an original idea must animate this nation and fresh currents of life must call into life fresh thoughts along its shores."[14] Thus far, Fuller argues in the same essay, American poetry is still largely imitative, no matter how skilled the American poets might be. Longfellow, for example, she finds to be pleasant and clever enough but lacking in the originality of imagination required of a genuine poet: "Nature with him, whether human or external, is always seen through the windows of literature."[15] To name the greatest poet of the day, the only one whose originality she can praise without qualification, Fuller has to turn to the English Wordsworth, a writer with the kind of intelligence "which can see the great in the little, and dignify the petty operations of Nature by tracing through them her most sublime principles."[16]

These convictions—about the potential of the country to produce a literature that is both original and respectably "classical" at the same time—Fuller carries with her on her tour of the Great Lakes as she examines the landscapes and the people, looking among the latter for signs of originality and instinctive response to the sublimity of the former. The white settlers, in general, she finds disappointing. They strike her as only transplanted Yankees who have brought with them their cautious habits and their acquisitiveness, and everywhere she looks, "the fatal spirit of imitation, of reference to European standards, penetrates, and threatens to blight whatever of original growth might adorn the soil" (62). Furthermore, in their haste to establish themselves and begin their prospering in the European mode, the new settlers appear oblivious to the natural beauty of the places where they choose to live. While a sensitive traveler who has come from afar to view the scene cannot help being awed by the beauty of the country, "most of these settlers do not see it at all; it breathes, it speaks in vain to those who are rushing into its sphere" (47). These white settlers, bent on clearing out the forests, making money, and imitating the Europeans, make it constantly difficult for Fuller to carry out her intention of looking on the meanness of the scene with an eye that can dignify it all by seeing the great in the little, the sublime in the petty.

To find the original idea, the germs of a new poetry, here on the edges of civilized America, Fuller must look outside the white settlements. When she does, she finds what she has been looking for (and was evidently prepared to find) in the camps of the Indians. The Indians are much easier to look at with the poetic eye than are the white settlers: they are themselves a unique feature of the American continent, and they do not imitate the Europeans. Perhaps most important for Fuller, the Indians—so she insists—have an instinctive aesthetic sense that gives them an appreciation for the beauty of nature, an appreciation so deep that it amounts to reverence. The visible evidence of the Indians' past habitations convinces Fuller that, unlike the white settlers, the Indians chose places to live because of the physical beauty of the site, and therefore they did not destroy the forests to make room for themselves: "They were the rightful lords of a beauty they forbore to deform" (47). Even the history of Indian warfare can be accounted for by reference to the Indian love of natural beauty: "How could they let themselves be conquered, with such a country to fight for!" (50). Having reached this conclusion, Fuller can do with her views of the Indians what she could not do with her views of the whites: she can look through the disappointing present and locate the buried sources of sublimity. The site of an ancient Indian village is enough to reassure her that she is right to trust her insight rather than her sight: "They may blacken Indian life as they will, talk of its dirt, its brutality, I will ever believe that the men who chose that dwelling-place were able to feel emotions of noble happiness as they returned to it, and so were the women that received them" (53).

In the Indians, then, Fuller discovers an original American subject and a fit object for the American poet's eye; she also finds in them more appropriate claimants to the American wilderness than the transplanted white settlers. However, in order to confer this new status on the Indians in a persuasive way, she must constantly remind the reader that the Indians of the present, the ones she actually encounters, are only living symbols or signifiers that must be *read* in the right way in order to understand where their appropriate referents are to be found:

> The men of these subjugated tribes, now accustomed to drunkenness and every way degraded, bear but a faint impress of the lost grandeur of the race. They are no longer strong, tall, or finely proportioned. Yet as you see them stealing along a height, or striding boldly forward, they remind you of what *was* majestic in the red man. (182)

To perceive the signs of majesty in the degraded Indians of the present may require a Wordsworthian originality of insight, an ability to read the traces of the sublime lingering on the degraded surface. Yet, to convey her perceptions, Fuller over and over does what she insists the American writer must not do: she goes directly to foreign models, and sees the Indians through the "windows of literature." Viewing a ruined Indian village, for example, "suggested to me a Greek splendor, a Greek sweetness, and I can believe that an Indian brave, accustomed to ramble in such paths, and be bathed by such sunbeams, might be mistaken for Apollo, as Apollo was for him by West" (53).[17] She observes one Indian man whose "air was French-Roman, that is, more romanesque than Roman," and another who "was not a French-Roman, but a real Roman" (120, 121). As she watches the Indians around their campfires on Mackinaw Island, she "wanted Sir Walter Scott to have been there," since he would have been able to "follow out the stories suggested by these weather-beaten, sullen, but eloquent figures" (174).

If the figures of the Indians are eloquent to Fuller, they are so only because she is able to refer them to a heroic past that is in every way different from their own past, to take them out of history and offer them to others (like Scott) who can resituate them in a *story* that she herself is not prepared to write. She does express her wish that someone will soon write a history of the Indians, but she has a significant stipulation: the historian should be someone "with his eye turned to the greatness of the past, rather than the scanty promise of the future" (232). Fuller's own eye is constantly turned to the past; the view of the present is disconcerting and baffling enough to make her conclude that the fate of the living Indians is already determined and that all talk of changing it must be a waste of words. The Indians of the present are a ragtag, coarse lot, a blight on the landscape. In the future they face only "speedy extinction" (234), as the example of the Cherokees in Georgia demonstrates; even if the Indians could produce their own leaders to act in their behalf, Fuller says, they would surely be "frustrated by the same barbarous self-ishness they were in Georgia. There was a chance of seeing what might have been done, now lost forever" (235). Whatever leaders the Indians might produce "have no more chance, than Julian in the times of old" (200).

Fuller even raises briefly the possibility of intermarriage between whites and Indians as an alternative to the extinction of the Indians, only to drop quickly into the most stereotypical kind of racist cliché and abandon the idea:

> Amalgamation would afford the only true and profound means of civilization. But nature seems, like all else, to declare, that this race

is fated to perish. Those of mixed blood fade early, and are not generally a fine race. They lose what is best in either type, rather than
enhance the value of each, by mingling. (195)

For Fuller, clearly, what is best in the Indian "type" is found only
in those Indians who have, *by dying*, made themselves available to
the poetic eye and the genteel imagination.

Fuller inserted into *Summer on the Lakes* a long summary account of a German book she had taken along on the trip with her.
The book, *The Seeress of Prevorst* (1831) by Justinus Kerner, details
the life of a young woman from the village of Prevorst, whose short
life was characterized (according to Kerner) by trances, out-of-body
experiences, communication with the dead, and susceptibility to the
"magnetic influences" of people, plants, animals, and inanimate objects. Fuller concludes her summary with an *apologia* that attempts
to justify her inclusion of this story of a German mystic in her own
account of life on the frontiers of midwestern America:

> Do not blame me that I have written so much about Germany and
> Hades, while you were looking for news of the West. Here, on the
> pier, I see disembarking the Germans, the Norwegians, the Swedes,
> the Swiss. Who knows how much of old legendary lore, of modern
> wonder, they have already planted amid the Wisconsin forests? Soon,
> soon their tales of the origin of things, and the Providence which rules
> them, will be so mingled with those of the Indians, that the very oak
> trees will not know them apart—will not know whether itself be a
> Runic, a Druid, or a Winnebago oak. (165)

Fuller places the story of the seeress among the folkloric baggage
that the European immigrants are daily bringing into frontier America. More important, she implies here that the mysticism of the
young German woman is consistent not only with the visionary
instincts of the native Indians but with her own desire to look
through the disturbing evidence of the material present and resituate
the Indians and the oak trees of America in a thoroughly aestheti-
cized, spiritualized, and exoticized past.

Fuller's implied conclusion is, finally, that the only Indian who
can be saved from extinction is the one whose body can be represented by the Apollo Belvedere and whose intelligence and beliefs

can be understood through an acquaintance with the mysticism of the Druids. And the only person who can save this Indian is the one who is able to perceive the traces of the sublime subtext through the degraded and distracting text of whatever the living Indian person might actually say or be:

> Although I have little to tell, I feel that I have learnt a great deal of the Indians, from observing them even in this broken and degraded condition. There is a language of eye and motion which cannot be put into words, and which teaches what words never can. I feel acquainted with the soul of this race; I read its nobler thought in their defaced figures. There *was* a greatness, unique and precious, which he who does not feel will never duly appreciate the majesty of nature in this American continent. (251)

This peroration suggests that Fuller has succeeded in the project she set for herself at the beginning of the narrative: to tease out the "mighty meaning" of the American frontier scene and to locate the springs of a new American poetry. They can both be found, she concludes, in the eloquent figure of the Indian, but only as that figure is "read" by the New Englander with a classical education, a Wordsworthian eye, an openness to mysticism, and a will to ennoble history by turning it into art. Such a person can preserve those images of the Indians that "will indicate as clearly their life, as a horse's head from the Parthenon the genius of Greece"(233).

Thoreau also traveled, like the other two writers, with the intention of exploring the frontier and reporting back to his untraveled readers, but he did not have to go as far as Fuller or Parkman did to do his reconnoitering. "The frontiers," he wrote in *A Week*, "are not east or west, north or south, but wherever a man *fronts* a fact. . . ."[18] Given this definition, then, Thoreau—that is, the Thoreau who is the "I" of his texts—is a perpetual frontiersman, one who is constantly turning his back on the habits of settled life to "front" those facts of the American landscape that the settlers are too preoccupied to see. A short walk from Concord to the Walden woods is all it takes for Thoreau to reach his frontier, to be in a place where there are new facts to be fronted: "I went to the woods because I wished to live deliberately, to front only the essential facts of life, and see if I could not learn what it had to teach. . . . "[19] That (frontier) act of confrontation with the essential is solitary and unmediated, by its nature; the challenge for Thoreau the writer is to reproduce the act within a text, using words that will become, for the reader, the equivalent of the facts that are one half of the frontier equation. If the words are right, and if the reader knows how to read, then the reading itself can be a frontier experience—a fronting of new and essential fact.

"I never read a novel," Thoreau says in *A Week,* "they have so little real life and thought in them. The reading which I love best is the scriptures of the several nations" (90). In his own writing, Thoreau sets out to at least begin providing the American nation with the scriptures it has never had, to represent in language what is most essential, most profound, and most worth valuing in American experience. The great problem of this project, a problem that Thoreau acknowledges indirectly, is to find an adequate language, one that can preserve the necessary immediacy of the "fronting" of fact and at the same time give it permanence within a written text. In *Walden,* Thoreau broaches the problem by distinguishing between spoken and written language, between the immediacy of hearing and the mediated experience of reading:

> The one is commonly transitory, a sound, a tongue, a dialect merely, almost brutish, and we learn it unconsciously, like the brutes, of our mothers. The other is the maturity and experience of that; if that is our mother tongue, this is our father tongue, a reserved and select expression, too significant to be heard by the ear, which we must be born again in order to speak.[20] (112)

Written language, the passage implies, is more highly evolved, more civilized, capable of more significant utterance than is spoken language. And yet it is also, Thoreau goes on to say, superior to all other sources of art because it is, paradoxically, the least artful: the written word "is the work of art nearest to life itself" (114).

These arguments about the superiority of written to spoken language are made in the chapter on "Reading"; in the following chapter, on "Sounds," Thoreau returns to the question of language, this time to remind his readers that, *as* readers, they are "in danger of forgetting the language which all things and events speak without metaphor, which alone is copious and standard" (122). The language without metaphor—spoken by owls, loons, trains, and church bells—is the language of unmediated aural experience: the mother tongue that we understand unconsciously, the dialect we share with the brute creation. In arguing in these two chapters that we must be receptive to both languages, the "copious" one that we absorb in infancy and the "select" one that we learn through mature thought, Thoreau is also reminding us of the intention of his own language: to translate the brutish mother tongue of immediate experience into the father tongue of civilized literature, a form of art that is closer than any other to life itself. His translations, that is, are meant to provide us with a language that has been raised above brutishness and transitoriness, and yet one in which we can still "front" life-as-fact.

Thoreau's argument about language is abstract and subjective enough to make it almost impossible for us to test it against the words he actually wrote, the sentences he constructed. The argument requires our attention, however, not because of whatever value it might have as a general theory of language, but because of what it tells us about the difficult (and, I believe, finally impossible) task Thoreau sets for himself in all his "frontier" writing—and therefore about the contradictions into which he was inevitably drawn. In the first place, we can see (if we do some translating of our own) that Thoreau's comments signal his effort to preserve the primitive and the transitory within a civilized, stable, written text, without letting either destroy what is essential in the other. In the second place, while Thoreau implies that such a text must somehow replicate the immediacy of the confrontation with primitive fact, must use the language that brings us *closest* to life, he also notes, without accounting for the contradiction, that the real value of both kinds of language he has discussed—the language of "Sounds" and the language of "Reading"—lies in their ability to *distance* us from what is immediately present. "All sound heard at the greatest possible distance," he says, "produces one and the same effect, a vibration of the universal lyre, just as the intervening atmosphere makes a distant ridge of earth interesting to our eyes by the azure tint it imparts to it" (*Walden*, 136). Similarly, when we sit down to read classical literature,

> life seems as still and serene as if it were very far off, and I believe it is not habitually seen from any common platform so truly and unexaggerated as in the light of literature. . . . Reading the classics, or conversing with those old Greeks and Latins in their surviving works, is like walking amid the stars and constellations, a high and by way serene to travel. (*A Week*, 296)

These apparent contradictions suggest that Thoreau wants his own use of language to convey both immediacy and distance at once, to allow the reader to confront the essential, individual fact and, in the same moment of reading, to listen to the universal lyre and walk among the stars.

In writing his American scriptures, Thoreau was aware that perhaps the most crucial figure in his texts was the American Indian, since it was the presence of the Indian that made American history and experience distinctive. But in his fascination with the Indians and in his efforts to write them into his scriptures, he runs into precisely the same contradiction that he does when he writes about language: he values the Indians for their primitiveness and their naturalness, which for Thoreau places them among the essential, unmediated "facts" of American life; but what actually attracts him most about the Indians is their *distance* from the realities of life in nineteenth-century America. That is, he would like the figure of the Indian to convey both immediacy and distance, to be one of the facts of American experience without really interfering in its material reality, to hunt in the real Maine woods (and haunt the Walden woods) and walk among the stars at the same time.

In *A Week*, which recounts Thoreau's travels in rural Massachusetts, he can declare that "our brave forefathers have exterminated all the Indians," doing the job so thoroughly that the "murmur of unchronicled nations has died away along these shores" (155, 328).

The absence of living Indians from the territory he travels through leaves Thoreau free in *A Week* to place the Indians, within his brief chronicle of American history,[21] just where he most wants them— at the distance of the stars:

> By the wary independence and aloofness of his dim forest life [the Indian] preserves his intercourse with his native gods, and is admitted from time to time to a rare and peculiar society with Nature. He has glances of starry recognition to which our saloons are strangers. The steady illumination of his genius, dim only because distant, is like the faint but satisfying light of the stars compared with the dazzling but ineffectual and short-lived blaze of candles. (69)

The starry, completely mythologized Indian, the embodiment of a primitive and instinctive reverence for what is wild and natural, suited Thoreau's purposes in *A Week* and in *Walden* completely— so completely that he could declare in *A Week* that "the Indian does well to continue Indian" (70).

That imagined Indian could be lyrically described in the father tongue, the language of literature. But Thoreau was also clearly fascinated by his real prototypes: the Indians who spoke the mother tongue and hunted real animals in real woods, the ones who left New England littered with the arrowheads that Thoreau was, by all accounts, so adept at finding. To discover remaining examples of those actual Indians, Thoreau had to look beyond Concord, Walden, and the riverbanks of Massachusetts; he looked constantly in his reading of history, as his "Indian books" and his journals indicate, and whenever he could, he looked at living Indian people.

What we find when we examine Thoreau's comments on Indians in the journals, however, is more contradiction; the mythologized Indian that Thoreau wanted and needed for his writing is there in the journals, but so are the living Indians whose fate was still being debated by white America, and what Thoreau has to say about the former is everywhere contradicted by what he has to say about the latter. For example, he writes that "the charm of the Indian to me is that he stands free and unconstrained in Nature," and again that the Indians "seem to me a distinct and equally respectable people, born to wander and to hunt, and not to be inoculated with the twilight civilization of the white man."[22] The appearance of "to me" in those two statements is telling; the Indian who charms Thoreau is the primitive hunter who wanders through the idealized "Nature" of Thoreau's literary imagination and who survives by being kept at a distance from white civilization—the one who does well to continue Indian.

On the other hand, when Thoreau takes up the very real matter of the ongoing displacement of Indians by whites, he has a very different thing to say about the Indian as hunter: "For the Indian there is no safety but in the plow. If he would not be pushed into the Pacific, he must seize hold of a plow-tail and let go his bow and arrow, his fish-spear and rifle" (1:444). On the matter of the removal of the Cherokees from Georgia, he is more specific, even blaming the Cherokees for being too slow about their assimilation into white civilization: "What detained the Cherokees so long was the 2923 plows which that people possessed; and if they had grasped their handles more firmly, they would never have been driven beyond the Mississippi" (1:446). In another place, Thoreau records his reactions on being shown an Indian pestle with a handle carved in the shape of a bird's head:

> But here an Indian has patiently sat and fashioned a stone into the likeness of a bird, and added some pure beauty to that pure utility, and so far begun to leave behind him war, and even hunting, and to redeem himself from the savage state. In this he was leaving off the savage. Enough of this would have saved him from extermination. (5:526)

This time Thoreau concludes that it is art rather than agriculture that could have saved the Indians by drawing them out of their savage hunter state, but in both of these cases his point is the same: the Indians condemned themselves by refusing to give up their primitive habits and adopt the habits of white civilization. And in both cases his comments are made in response to the hard facts of political and historical reality, a reality to which the mythologized Indian, the one who "stands free and unconstrained in Nature," is largely irrelevant.

There are two other entries in the journals that illustrate more concretely the difficulty Thoreau had in reconciling "the Indian" of his imagination with the actual Indian people still living in America. In July of 1850 he set down this picture of an Indian woman whom he may or may not have actually seen: "A lone Indian woman without children, accompanied by her dog, wearing the shroud of her race, performing the last offices for her departed race. Not yet absorbed into the elements again; a daughter of the soil; one of the nobility of the land" (2:42). Six years later he provides another portrait of an Indian woman, this time one he deliberately went looking for so that he could observe her and talk to her:

> Heard of, and sought out, the hut of Martha Simons, the only pure-blooded Indian left about New Bedford. . . . She had a peculiarly vacant expression, perhaps characteristic of the Indian, and answered our questions listlessly, without being interested or implicated, mostly in monosyllables, as if hardly present there. To judge from her physiognomy, she might have been King Philip's own daughter. Yet she could not speak a word of Indian, and knew nothing of her race." (8:390–91)

The image of the Indian woman as a silent priestess, the last scion of a race of noble primitives, does not survive the long trip to the real hut of Martha Simons. It might have survived if Martha Simons had only remained silent, since her appearance ("physiognomy") allows Thoreau to see her, as he saw the first woman, as the daughter of Indian nobility; once she begins to speak in listless English, however, admitting that she does not speak "Indian," she separates herself from her exotic "race," and Thoreau is no longer very interested.

All of these journal entries were recorded before Thoreau made his third trip to Maine, in July of 1857. When he returned from that trip, he wrote a letter in which he suggests that he had finally found what he had been looking for in his previous trips as well as in his writing about Indians. What he found in the Indian guide Joe Polis, he says in the letter, was "an intelligent Indian." The trip took him into "the new world which the Indian dwells in, or is," and taught him that "intelligence flows in other channels than I knew. It redeems for me portions of what seemed brutish before."[23] In Polis, that is, Thoreau claims to have found a person who allows him to merge the two images of the Indians that he had not been able to reconcile in the journals. Polis sits in the same canoe with Thoreau and sleeps by the same fire, while still convincing Thoreau that he is completely other, the inhabitant of a different world; he can be, that is, both immediately present to Thoreau and distant at the same time. Most important, Polis's "intelligence" redeems him from "brutishness," thereby letting him become for Thoreau a human embodiment of the kind of successful merger he had theorized about in his discussions of language in *Walden*. In fact, as we shall see, it was largely because of Polis's bilingualism, his ability to speak both English and his native Penobscot dialect, that Thoreau was able to see him as redeeming his Indian brutishness through his intelligence.

On his first trip to Maine, in 1846 ("Ktaadn"), the only person Thoreau finds whose "general intelligence" is worth remarking is a white man, the retired waterman McCauslin (24). The Indian town he visits near Oldtown discourages Thoreau because its buildings are too shabby and its inhabitants too much engaged with the modern world: "These were once a powerful tribe. Politics are all the rage with them now" (7). The Indians he encounters beyond the town are also thoroughly disappointing, and Thoreau's response to them is predictive of his reaction to Martha Simons ten years later:

> Met face to face, these Indians in their native woods looked like the sinister and slouching fellows whom you meet picking up strings and paper in the streets of a city. There is, in fact, a remarkable and unexpected resemblance between the degraded savage and the lowest classes in a great city. The one is no more a child of nature than the other. (86)

In this first account, the only Indian who can be redeemed from degradation and brutishness and restored to his role as a "child of nature" is the one Thoreau conjures up in his imagination and sets at the greatest possible distance from himself. This one is "a more ancient and primitive man" than the slouching fellows he meets "face to face." He is "but dim and misty to me" as he paddles up the river of Thoreau's imagination and is soon "lost to my sight, as a more distant and misty cloud is seen flitting by behind a nearer, and is lost in space. So he goes about his destiny, the red face of man" (87, 88).

On the second trip, in 1853 ("Chesuncook"), Thoreau spends more time with Indians than he had on the first, traveling with an Indian guide named Joe Aitteon and sharing a hunting camp for a while with a group of Joe's friends. This time Thoreau watches and listens to the Indians carefully, as if he is bent on being able to attach "the red face of man" to the body of one of his real Indian companions. His reactions this time are more thoughtful, less prefabricated than they were on the first trip, but the pattern of response is finally the same. He is unpleasantly surprised, for example, to hear Aitteon singing "O Susanna" and saying, repeatedly, "Yes, Sir-ee" (119), and it is Aitteon's tracking and slaughtering of a moose that leads Thoreau to the conclusion that Indians make a "coarse and imperfect use" of nature. He calls the moose-killing a "tragedy" and regrets his own part in it, which, he says, "as it affected the innocence, destroyed the pleasure of my adventure" (132). Joe Aitteon not only refuses to be the savage innocent; he refuses to be *either* very savage or very innocent. To Thoreau's mind, only the color of Joe's skin distinguishes him from the loutish white lumbermen who are destroying the forest.

There is, however, one moment in "Chesuncook" when Thoreau seems to have found what he came looking for in the Indians. The moment occurs in his description of a night spent in the Indians' hunting camp. Having first spread his blanket over the moose hides provided by the Indians, "for fear of dirt," Thoreau lies awake listening to Joe and his friends talk in their native dialect. Hearing this unintelligible speech, which he is convinced has not undergone the "change and deterioration" that is apparent to him in all other aspects of Indian life, restores Thoreau's confidence in a genuinely aboriginal race that is not "the invention of historians and poets." The speech that Thoreau hears is a species of the mother tongue of *Walden*, the "copious" language without metaphor of "Sounds":

> It was a purely wild and primitive American sound, as much as the barking of a chickaree, and I could not understand a syllable of it. . . .

These Abenakes gossiped, laughed, and jested, in the language in which Eliot's Indian Bible is written, the language which has been spoken in New England who shall say how long? These were the sounds that issued from the wigwams of this country before Columbus was born; they have not yet died away; and, with remarkably few exceptions, the language of their forefathers is still copious for them. I felt that I stood, or rather lay, as near to the primitive man of America, that night, as any of its discoverers did. (151)

Thoreau seems to have found his primitive Indian here, lying right next to him in the Maine woods. However, no matter how close the man Joe Aitteon may be lying, the primitive man is still as misty and dim as the imagined one of the "Ktaadn" narrative: Thoreau finds him only in the dark when he listens rather than looks, and, significantly, only when what he hears is unintelligible. What Thoreau discovers is a disembodied and moveable sound, to which he can attach the significance he would like it to have. By daylight, the sound will degenerate into the voice of Joe Aitteon, who speaks in broken, backwoods English, sings Stephen Foster songs, and threatens, by his sheer coarseness, to destroy Thoreau's innocent pleasure in the woods.

It is only on his third trip, in July of 1857 ("The Allegash and East Branch"), that Thoreau finds, in Joe Polis, the man he can call the "intelligent Indian." If we examine his reactions to Polis, however, we see that what Thoreau really finds is an *intelligible* Indian, one who can illustrate for Thoreau "that strange remoteness in which the Indian ever dwells to the white man" (175) while at the same time willingly agreeing to Thoreau's proposal that "I would tell him all I knew, and he should tell me all he knew" (186). Polis and Thoreau school each other, Thoreau collecting the Indian names of things and asking their meaning, and Polis collecting the white man's wisdom: "The Indian asked the meaning of *reality*, as near as I could make out the word, which he said one of us had used; also of '*interrent*,' that is, intelligent" (187). The two men translate the world for each other, Polis providing words from his language to name animals, plants, lakes, and mountains, and Thoreau providing words from his language to convey abstract ideas. The Indian knows the reality of his world minutely, at first hand, but he needs the white

man (according to Thoreau) to synthesize for him—to explain that
what he knows is *reality*, and that his knowing it so well makes him
intelligent. Taken together, then, the discourses of the two men come
close to constituting that ideal (and intelligible) utterance that Thoreau had sought to define in *Walden*: the abstract, literary father
tongue in which the almost brutish dialect of the mother tongue can
still be heard.[24]

In the narrative of this third trip, Thoreau describes an episode
that closely resembles his account of listening to the conversation of
Joe Aitteon and his friends in the second narrative. This episode also
occurs at night, in a tent in the woods, and again Thoreau listens in
silence to the sounds of an Indian language. But there are some very
significant differences between the two accounts: this time Polis sings
rather than conversing; his song is "a very simple religious exercise
or hymn, the burden of which was, that there was only one God who
ruled all the world"; and, most important, Polis translates the hymn
into English after he has sung it. Listening to Polis sing, Thoreau is
again transported back into the past, as he was when he listened to
Aitteon and his friends, but this time the image of the past has
changed:

> His singing carried me back to the period of the discovery of America,
> to San Salvador and the Incas, when Europeans first encountered the
> simple faith of the Indian. There was, indeed, a beautiful simplicity
> about it; nothing of the dark and savage, only the mild and infantile.
> The sentiments of humility and reverence chiefly were expressed.
> (198)

Because Polis's words are translated into English, making his song
intelligible, and because the meaning of his song is familiar rather
than exotic, his primitive language redeems what before was brutish,
translating the savage into the infantile. The song, in effect, makes
the Indian himself intelligible to Thoreau.

On his second Maine trip, Thoreau expresses his surprise (as he
does in his journal description of Martha Simons) that the Indians
"knew but little of the history of their race" (150). To a great extent,
Thoreau's interest in the Indians in *The Maine Woods* is directed

toward finding a way of understanding the history of their "race," a way of making the Indian past intelligible and *usable* to one who would like to provide contemporary America with its scriptures. He seems to have found an entry into the history he is looking for through Joe Polis, the Indian whose manner and language allow Thoreau to see his racial origins as "mild and infantile," rather than "dark and savage." But if Polis is the representative of the Indian past made intelligible to the white writer, he has little relevance to the present or the future—except as he is usable to the writer. Having discovered Polis in the backwoods of Maine, Thoreau returns to Concord to record one more "fact" about Indians in his journal for January 1858:

> Who can doubt that men are by a certain fate what they are . . . ? Who can doubt this essential and innate difference between man and man, when he considers a whole new race, like the Indian, inevitably and resignedly passing away in spite of our efforts to Christianize and educate them? Individuals accept their fate and live according to it, as the Indian does. Everybody notices that the Indian retains his habits wonderfully,—is still the same man that the discoverers found. The fact is, the history of the white man is a history of improvement, that of the red man a history of fixed habits of stagnation. (10:35–52)

Many of the tag words that characterize the rhetoric of nineteenth-century debates on the Indians are there in this entry—*fate, educate, Christianize, improvement, stagnation, passing away*—written only four months after Thoreau made his study of Joe Polis, a Christian Indian who could read English and whose son, we are told, "was the best scholar in the school at Oldtown, to which he went with whites" (323).

Thoreau clearly went to Maine to find in the deep woods the same man that "the discoverers found," not to learn what life might be like in 1857 for the Indian community in and around Oldtown (where the children went to school and the adults took an interest in local and national politics). Having persuaded himself that the primitive man could still be found in the nighttime woods, Thoreau could then come home to declare the truth about Indian history: it is static, the Indians have learned nothing from the whites (since the *true* Indian is still a primitive), and they are therefore fated to become extinct. The only trouble was, he couldn't publish what he learned by observing Polis in the woods. Joe Polis might read the article, might even confront Thoreau about its political implications. That complicated everything.

As we have seen, both Fuller and Thoreau avoid any but the most cursory consideration of the political and practical questions raised by the condition of the Indians in the United States, since both seem fully persuaded that there is no alternative to the future extinction of the Indians. For both these writers, the implications of the "Indian question" are almost entirely aesthetic and literary: if American literature must incorporate the Indians in order to be authentically American, and both writers seem to agree that it must, then what shape ought the textualized Indian to take? How is the "uncivilized" Indian to be made intelligible (that is, readable) to an eastern audience that is impatient for the civilizing of American literature to proceed? As we have also seen, Fuller and Thoreau answer the question by insisting that America must send its poets out to the deep woods and the frontiers to interpret the Indians for contemporary readers and preserve them for future readers and writers. Fuller and Thoreau find the living Indians they encounter intelligible only to the eye (and, in Thoreau's case, the ear) of the poet, who can accomplish the difficult task of translating all American Indians into "the Indian," a figure fit for readers to encounter within a civilized American text.

Francis Parkman also set out, as an aspiring historian, to make the Indians intelligible to his readers, but Parkman was persuaded that the American public misunderstood the Indians precisely because it had thus far allowed itself to be duped by the poets and fiction writers. He makes his position clear early in *The Conspiracy of Pontiac*:

> Of the Indian character, much has been written foolishly, and credulously believed. By the rhapsodies of poets, the cant of sentimentalists, and the extravagances of some who should have known better, a counterfeit image has been tricked out, which might seek in vain for

its likeness through every corner of the habitable earth; an image bearing no more resemblance to its original than the monarch of the tragedy and the hero of the epic poem bear to their living prototypes in the palace and the camp. The shadows of his wilderness home, and the darker mantle of his own inscrutable reserve, have made the Indian warrior a wonder and a mystery. Yet to the eye of rational observation there is nothing unintelligible in him.[25]

For Parkman, it is not the impressionable poet's eye but "the eye of rational observation" that can make the Indian intelligible and situate him in his proper place in the history of the country.

While Fuller and Thoreau are concerned with making the American past available for American writers, Parkman is equally concerned with rescuing it from both the local poets and the foreign historians. In the preface to *The Conspiracy of Pontiac*, Parkman suggests that the writing of American history is itself a kind of frontier activity, requiring the same resourcefulness and vigor that the successful American pioneer needs. "The field of the history," Parkman says of his own writing project, "was uncultured and unreclaimed, and the labour that awaited me was like that of the border settler, who, before he builds his rugged dwelling, must fell the forest-trees, burn the undergrowth, clear the ground, and hew the fallen trunks to due proportion" (1:xxxiii). By offering this image of his labors as a writer, Parkman separates himself from the poets and makes a claim for the greater immediacy and accuracy of his work, attributing to himself by implication the same kind of "manly directness" he admired in the novels of Cooper.[26] And yet, as we shall see, in presenting his portrait of Pontiac, Parkman falls back on exactly the kind of useful literary models that he wishes to reject; to make his Pontiac intelligible, that is, he chooses to cast him as a tragic hero.

In using the metaphor of the frontiersman clearing out a place for his habitation, Parkman implies that his history (as he would like the reader to see it) is as plain and unadorned as the "rugged dwelling" of the frontier settler. At the same time, the very fact that he launches the history with an elaborate metaphor suggests that he is being careful to make his "dwelling" attractive and comfortable as well as serviceable. The use of this particular metaphor suggests, in other words, that Parkman is aiming at the same combination of qualities in this book for which a reviewer had praised his writing in *The Oregon Trail*: Parkman's narrative, the reviewer wrote, "has all the air of truth with the attractiveness of fiction."[27] As David Levin has pointed out, Parkman was one of those nineteenth-century historians (Levin's other examples are Bancroft, Prescott, and Motley) who "concentrated on literary technique, 'interest,' and effect not only because they had been literary men before they became historians, but also because they believed that the re-creation of the Past requires imaginative and literary skill."[28]

The question for Parkman, then, is essentially the same one confronted by Fuller and Thoreau, the one American critics had been debating for years: How does one give an accurate picture of the Indians while at the same time producing a text that will be aesthetically pleasing to a well-read audience? We know that Parkman made his trip west on the Oregon Trail to help insure the accuracy of his portrait of the Indians in *The Conspiracy of Pontiac*, and that *The Oregon Trail* was in this sense a by-product of his research for the history book. However, we can also see in retrospect that by writing the travel narrative, Parkman was preparing his audience as well as himself for the magisterial history to follow. In *The Oregon Trail*, Parkman confronts the living Indians of the Far West, whom he finds to be "thorough savages, unchanged by any contact with civilization" (160), and performs on them the same operation he described himself as performing on the "crude and promiscuous" materials of the history book: he hews them down to manageable proportions to make them usable for the construction of the history.

In *The Conspiracy of Pontiac*, Parkman announces that his intent is "to portray the American forest and the American Indian at the period when both received their final doom" (1:xxxi). He is not at all hesitant in this book to collapse everything he knows (or believes) about Indians into a portrait of the generic "American Indian" and to generalize about the characteristics of that monolithic figure. At the same time, the things Parkman knows about his generic Indian make it difficult to enclose him within a text that is governed by

traditional literary conventions, since his Indian is the very embodiment of lawlessness and resistance to forms: "A wild love of liberty,
an utter intolerance of control, lie at the basis of his character, and
fire his whole existence" (1:31). As a group, the Indians are "unstable
as water, capricious as the winds," acting at times "like ungoverned
children fired with the instincts of devils" (2:186). This unrestrained,
unstable Indian can be as much a threat to the stability of a formal
text as he is to the safety of the settlements of white civilization. In
this book, Parkman manages the problem of representing the lawless
Indian by stabilizing his image in Pontiac, the archetypical Indian
who can stand in for all others; Pontiac "was a thorough savage, and
in him stand forth, in strongest light and shadow, the native faults
and virtues of the Indian race" (1:168). Furthermore, Parkman casts
Pontiac in a role that makes him both intelligible to readers and useful
as a means of organizing the text in a conventional way. Because
Pontiac illustrates so markedly and forcefully both the faults and the
virtues of the defeated race he represents, Parkman can declare him
a tragic hero—"the savage hero of this dark forest tragedy" (1:187).

Through his treatment of Pontiac, therefore, Parkman converts
the opaque, savage other into the familiar, readable tragic hero, a
stabilized figure to whom his audience will already know how to
respond. To accomplish this conversion, he supplies Pontiac with the
characteristics that conventional tragedy usually requires of the hero,
the combination of virtues and faults that will allow the reader to
admire and envy his strengths while at the same time accepting the
inevitability of his failure. Pontiac's most damning fault is easily
stated: he "will not learn the arts of civilization, and he and his forest
must perish together." In his wildness, Pontiac is almost indistinguishable from the forest he inhabits, and even as Parkman goes
about his clearing and hewing as the pioneer/historian, he notes that
"we look with deep interest on the fate of this irreclaimable son of
the wilderness" as his doom approaches.

> And our interest increases when we discern in the unhappy wanderer,
> mingled among his vices, the germs of heroic virtues—a hand boun-
> tiful to bestow, as it is rapacious to seize, and, even in extremest

famine, imparting its last morsel to a fellow-sufferer; a heart which, strong in friendship as in hate, thinks it not too much to lay down life for its chosen comrade; a soul true to its own idea of honour, and burning with an unquenchable thirst for greatness and renown. (1: 32–33)

These are *Indian* versions of generosity, loyalty, honor, and ambition, and therefore present only as the "germs" of genuinely heroic virtue, but they are sufficient to allow Parkman to justify asking his audience for the requisite sympathy for his tragic hero.

In the course of making Pontiac intelligible to the reader, Parkman is at the same time making the whole course of Indian-white relations in America intelligible. Pontiac becomes tractable enough to inhabit a civilized text once he is shaped into a conventional tragic hero, which means, of course, that he must also be a doomed hero. For Parkman, this version of Pontiac's history provides a model for scripting the entire story of the American Indians' confrontation with white civilization: "To reclaim the Indians from their savage state has again and again been attempted, and each attempt has failed. Their intractable, unchanging character leaves no other alternative than their gradual extinction, or the abandonment of the western world to eternal barbarism" (2:101). Either the Indians survive, or the forms of Western civilization—including its forms of tragedy and historiography—survive; for Parkman, the two clearly cannot exist simultaneously.

The Conspiracy of Pontiac was written at a distance, temporal and geographical, from the Indians who are Parkman's primary subjects. *The Oregon Trail*, on the other hand, is Parkman's reconstruction of his actual encounters with living Indians west of the Mississippi. The account was first published serially in the *Knickerbocker Magazine* (February 1847–February 1849) under the title "The Oregon Trail. Or a Summer's Journey Out of Bounds. By A Bostonian." The fact that a magazine located in New York City would carry the account in twenty-one installments, over two years, is one measure of the interest that had been generated in the East by the opening of routes across the continent to the West Coast. The first mass movement to Oregon had taken place in 1843, and by the spring of 1846, when Parkman began his trip, the supporters of the annexation of Oregon had done so much effective lobbying that thousands of emigrants were collecting at the eastern end of the trail, waiting for the snow to melt so that they could begin their trek toward the promised riches of the Oregon territory.[29] Although readers in the East knew, therefore, that streams of people were crossing the trail in the summer of 1846, Parkman's original title suggests that he (and the editors of the *Knickerbocker Magazine*) assumed that for a literate, educated Bostonian to be among the emigrants on the trail was an anomaly; among all those travelers, he alone was "out of bounds." The title also suggests that the narrative itself has been written with the consciousness that it is not bounded in the way that other texts are. As a compilation of frontier travel notes, that is, *The Oregon Trail* need not conform to any traditional literary conventions to attract readers and gain their confidence. In fact, the more such a text exceeds the bounds of convention, the more likely the audience will be to accept the authenticity of its firsthand account of the lawless frontier, a place where the intrepid traveler finds, Parkman says, that "the whole fabric of art and conventionality is struck rudely to pieces" (105).

In this out-of-bounds text, a text ungoverned by literary convention, Parkman does not need to turn the Indians into readable characters who can be fitted into a familiar pattern; he is free to let them remain as ungoverned and lawless as the text they inhabit. His purpose here is not, as it is in *The Conspiracy of Pontiac*, to make the Indians and their history intelligible "to the eye of rational observation." Here, instead, Parkman begins preparing himself and his readers for that subsequent massive act of interpretation by confronting the living, ungovernable Indians and declaring them unfit, in every way, to inhabit a civilized, governed text. For Parkman, there are no conventions that allow us to "read" the living Indians in any coherent or satisfying way. (At one point in *The Oregon Trail*, as Parkman describes his first view of Pike's Peak, he inserts into the text a stanza from Byron's "Childe Harold" describing a desolate mountain scene. The lines from the poem would be "verified" by the actual scene he is looking at, Parkman says, except for one crucial omission; in the poem there are no "fierce savages, restlessly wandering through summer and winter" [373]. Those savages exist outside the bounds of poetry.) His purpose in *The Oregon Trail*, then, is to begin a preliminary clearing out of the living Indians, who are both unaesthetic and unintelligible, as a necessary preparation for making them readable—intelligible and aesthetically pleasing—through the conventions of interpretation he provides in *The Conspiracy of Pontiac.*

Although Parkman's descriptions of Indians in *The Oregon Trail* are taken from firsthand observation of a number of different tribes, living in varying degrees of proximity to white settlements, and although he is attentive to local variations in such matters as dress and eating habits, the differences he notes still do not prevent him from attaching his conclusions to the generic figure of "the Indian." He defends himself, indirectly, by pointing out that where the "mental features" of Indians are concerned, "the same picture, slightly changed in shade and coloring, would serve with very few exceptions for all the tribes that lie north of the Mexican territories" (251). Ironically, the characteristic that Parkman finds common to all Indians, sufficiently common that it allows him to generalize, is their unpredictability—their constant refusal to act in ways that are intelligible to the white observer; "my own observation," Parkman says, "had taught me the extreme folly of confidence, and the utter impossibility of foreseeing to what sudden acts the strange unbridled impulses of an Indian may urge him" (328). This impulsiveness of Indian behavior he attributes in part to their innate "mental features" and in part to the indulgence with which Indian parents rear their children, a practice "which tends not a little to foster that wild idea of liberty and utter intolerance of restraint which lie at the very foundation of the Indian character" (294). Even when an Indian addresses a white man with specific information to convey—as happens when a man Parkman calls The Stabber sits him down to tell him some news—his discourse is so undisciplined and impulsive as to be incomprehensible. The story told by The Stabber, Parkman says, "was so entangled, like the greater part of an Indian's stories, with absurd and contradictory details, that it was almost impossible to disengage from it a single particle of truth" (361).

The unpredictability of the Indians, their complete otherness, makes them lively and picturesque subjects for a travel narrative; at one point, as Parkman describes the scene of an Indian encampment on the move, he even echoes Fuller in pleading that "only the pen of a Scott could have done it justice in description" (344). For Parkman, however, the Indians' unpredictability is also what makes them dangerous to the unsuspecting whites who cross their paths: "When among this people danger is never so near as when you are unprepared for it, never so remote as when you are armed and on the alert to meet it at any moment" (328). His own rifle, Parkman keeps reminding us, was always at the ready, and his prairie motto was " *'Semper Paratus'* " (201). His account of Indian nature, therefore, supplies him with a justification for saying that anyone whose travels out of bounds take him into Indian territory must be prepared to kill Indians in self-defense. But Parkman goes much further than this, also supplying himself (and his readers) with reasons for *wanting* to kill Indians.

The one completely unredeemable fact about Indians for Parkman, the feature that makes them not only exotic but killable, is that they are physically ugly. His narrative is peppered with gratuitous comments on the ugliness of the Indians he encounters, especially the women. Entering an Indian camp he notices "the old women, ugly as Macbeth's witches" (141); in another place he sees "a hideous, emaciated old woman" (162), and in yet another "a hideous old hag of eighty. Human imagination never conceived hobgoblin or witch more ugly than she" (196). The squaws in general are "maudlin" creatures, surrounded by "their mongrel progeny" (169, 181). Although the men receive less attention, they are clearly offensive as well, their ugliness sometimes being the one thing Parkman remembers about them: "An Indian went with us, whose name I forget, though the ugliness of his face and the ghastly width of his mouth dwell vividly in my recollection" (347). Among the Arapahoes, Parkman says, "I looked in vain . . . to discover one manly or

generous expression; all were wolfish, sinister, and malignant, and
their complexions, as well as their features, unlike those of the Dahcotah, were exceedingly bad" (398).

Parkman constantly reads these faces, seeing in their physical
difference (which he perceives as ugliness) signs of their moral difference (which he perceives as inferiority). The physical differences
between himself and the Indians are great enough to allow him to
declare the Indians less than fully human, and therefore dispensable.
Here is his description of one of the few Indians he did not despise,
a man Parkman calls the Panther:

> He had not the same features with those of other Indians. Unless his
> handsome face greatly belied him, he was free from the jealousy,
> suspicion and malignant cunning of his people. For the most part, a
> civilized white man can discover but very few points of sympathy
> between his own nature and that of an Indian. With every disposition
> to do justice to their good qualities, he must be conscious that an
> impassable gulf lies between him and his red brethren of the prairie.
> Nay, so alien to himself do they appear, that having breathed for a
> few months or a few weeks the air of this region, he begins to look
> upon them as a troublesome and dangerous species of wild beast, and
> if expedient, he could shoot them with as little compunction as they
> themselves would experience after performing the same office upon
> him. Yet, in the countenance of the Panther, I gladly read that there
> were at least some points of sympathy between him and me. (336–
> 37)

The point of sympathy and of moral correspondence between the
Panther and Parkman can be read in the handsome face of the Indian;
because he is not offensive to the eyes of the "civilized white man,"
he does not tempt Parkman to shoot him, as his uglier kinsmen do.

Parkman's attitude toward the physical appearance of the Indians
is exactly paralleled by his attitude toward the animals of the prairies:
he enjoys shooting the ugly ones, and feels some "civilized" remorse
about shooting the prettier ones. When he first shoots an antelope,
for example, the "expiring eye" of the animal gives him pause: "It
was like a beautiful woman's, dark and rich. 'Fortunate that I am in
a hurry,' thought I; 'I might be troubled with remorse, if I had time

for it' " (187). The buffalo, on the other hand, are a different matter. Because they are ugly, Parkman kills them (as often as he can) with an almost ecstatic pleasure: "No man who has not experienced it, can understand with what keen relish one inflicts his death wound, with what profound contentment of mind he beholds him fall" (418). Watching a group of buffalo bulls, Parkman addresses them mentally: " 'You are too ugly to live,' thought I; and aiming at the ugliest, I shot three of them in succession" (440). That same impulse to kill what is ugly, and that same anticipation of pleasure in the killing, characterizes his response to the "ugly" Indians—a response about which Parkman is startlingly blunt. He offers no apology for this description of his reaction to an old medicine man he watched,

> who with his hard, emaciated face and gaunt ribs was perched aloft like a turkey-buzzard, among the dead branches of an old tree, constantly on the look-out for enemies. He would have made a capital shot. A rifle bullet, skilfully planted, would have brought him tumbling to the ground. Surely, I thought, there could be no more harm in shooting such a hideous old villain, to see how ugly he would look when he was dead, than in shooting the detestable vulture which he resembled. (225)

Only ten pages after this passage, Parkman again describes his shooting of an antelope, and again the "glistening eyes" of the beautiful animal are so affecting that "it was with feelings of infinite compunction that I shot him through the head with a pistol" (235).

Parkman's language in these descriptions constitutes an explicit invitation to the reader to see the ugly animals, the buffalo and the vulture, as surrogates for the ugly Indians. In killing the animals, he is also symbolically killing the Indians, not just because it is pleasurable to rid the landscape of such blighting ugliness but also because the ugliness itself threatens to destroy whatever is beautiful in the landscape. (The violence against the Indians was, of course, not entirely symbolic, since in wantonly killing buffalo for the sheer pleasure of it, Parkman and his companions were helping to deprive the Indians of their most important food source.)[30] In Parkman's final account of a buffalo hunt, he also includes one final encounter with an antelope, this time one that approaches as he lies waiting for a good shot at a bull: "By the side of the shaggy and brutish monsters before me, it seemed like some lovely young girl wandering near a den of robbers or a nest of bearded pirates. The buffalo looked uglier than ever" (441).

As a Bostonian traveling out of bounds on the prairies, Parkman registers his disgust with all that offends him morally and aesthetically and freely acknowledges that his disgust is great enough to give him pleasure in the literal killing of animals and the symbolic or imagined killing of Indians. Out on the prairies, where "conventionality" has no relevance, such killing can be justified on both moral and aesthetic grounds. Similarly, as a writer traveling out of bounds in order to prepare himself for writing a book that will be bounded by convention, Parkman begins in *The Oregon Trail* the process of clearing the "uncultured and unreclaimed" field that he speaks of in the preface to *The Conspiracy of Pontiac*, destroying what is unusable and hewing the rest down "to due proportion." The most crucial part of that process is his "killing" of the ugly, unrestrained, and unpredictable Indians in order to make them available to the conventions of tragedy, thereby making them intelligible to a conventional reading. For Parkman, as we have seen, the live Indian and the savage hero of the forest tragedy cannot coexist. In the travel narrative, then, Parkman begins clearing the ground for his habitation as interpretive historian; by ridding that ground of living savages, he not only insures the aesthetic integrity of the civilized text to follow but also makes it possible for his readers to come with him into the cleared space in complete comfort and safety.

Conclusion

IN RECENT YEARS, American literary critics have been turning their attention more and more to the project of identifying and examining the various cultural myths that have seemed to dominate the canon of our national literature. The literature of the nineteenth century has been an especially fertile ground for the myth-seeking critic, since the canon of American literature has always been essentially a nineteenth-century canon. Having become aware of how extensively our contemporary society and even our individual lives have been shaped and delimited by certain hegemonic myths, especially the interdependent myths of patriarchy, of white supremacy, and of "manifest destiny," we have gone back to the canonical texts to locate the origins and trace the life-cycles of these myths. And we have been rewarded in our search: energized by our new insights, we have been able to find, almost anywhere we look, evidence of the blindness of nineteenth-century writers to their complicity in the perpetuation of those myths that can now seem to us both so naive and so damaging in their effects on American culture. My own project in this book could be described, to use my term, as part of this larger project of myth-seeking, since I have attempted to make a case for the susceptibility of many (even most) nineteenth-century American writers to the dominant myths of American nation-building, with their inherent discriminations between those who are eligible for citizenship within the nation and those who are not.

In speaking of myth here, I am adopting Roland Barthes's definition of myth as "depoliticized speech" and accepting his characterization of myth as a discourse that "transforms history into nature." With the exception of Melville, all the writers I discuss in the preceding chapters are, as I read them, specifically working to produce a discourse that can be taken as apolitical. (I exempt Melville from this generalization because I see his fiction as, in one sense, a record of his *resistance* to the depoliticizing of American literary discourse.) For the fiction writers, this means setting their fiction against history, making implicit claims for its very lack of historicity as justification for its value as a corrective to history. For the travel writers, on the other hand, the project is not to correct history so much as it is to replace it, as a distinctive category of experience or of discourse, with nature. History becomes growth, and travel to an American frontier becomes a means of observing the growth in those places where it is most unencumbered, most perceptibly "natural."

Barthes cites the universalizing myth of "the great family of man," with its emphasis on the commonality of certain human experiences, as one of the most innocuous seeming and most seductive of the myths that "transform history into nature." In this myth, Barthes says, "what could originally pass for a phrase belonging to zoology . . . is here amply moralized and sentimentalized." The latent intent of the myth, according to Barthes, is to "suppress the determining weight of History" so that we recognize only similarities and not differences; we are prevented by sentimentality from looking through the figure of the family and into the "zone" behind it "where historical alienation introduces some 'differences' which we shall here quite simply call 'injustices.' "[1]

I refer to Barthes's identification of the family myth because I want to suggest its usefulness as one way of understanding the kinds of discourse generated by white America's efforts to find a comfortable and justifiable position vis-à-vis the Indians. It is clearly no accident that in so much nineteenth-century writing the Indians are represented in family terms, such as "our red brothers," "God's red children," and "the sons of Adam." The family language serves as a means of eliding those differences in ethnicity, social organization, belief, and behavior that are so patently at the heart of the problem of Indian-white incompatibility. The concept of the family-of-man myth is particularly useful, I believe, if, taking Barthes as a starting point, we go beyond his characterization of the myth as blocking our perceptions of injustice and consider what happens when the myth is used to produce a model for the political organization of the country—that is, for the "nation." To figure the nation as a family, especially in an era in many ways uncritical of patriarchy, is to depoliticize questions of power and to naturalize social and political hierarchies. Within the mythic family, organization is natural, changes are evolutionary and teleological, and relationships are ultimately regulated by goodwill and affection. There are no outsiders, and even the most recalcitrant child eventually realizes that parents use power for the good of their offspring.

Most of the writers discussed in this book use, or at least invoke, the family myth as a way of reconceiving difference—even of reconceiving the political problems raised by the heterogeneity of the population of North America. Among the fiction writers, the family myth is used most overtly and extensively by Catherine Sedgwick and Lydia Maria Child, whose work is addressed to a largely female audience and who might therefore be confident of their audience's receptivity to the model of the family as a way of figuring social and political relationships. For them, the crucial question of how Indian and white people are going to share the American nation becomes reimagined as a question about how to move the Indians into the American family, where they can be nurtured into mature citizenship. Having raised and then rejected the possibility of miscegenated marriage, both women choose instead the vaguer (and more depoliticized) model of the adoption of the Indian into a woman-centered household.

Melville also draws on the family myth for models, although his models are, as I have suggested in Chapter 2, thoroughly ironized. Only his most self-deluding characters, those most given to wishful thinking, are capable of taking the family myth seriously as a guide to thinking. Both Captain Delano and the narrator of "Bartleby," for example, comfort themselves with an image of the family household at those moments when they are most disconcerted by their confrontations with others who are radically different from themselves and by their intimations that the spaces between themselves and the others are hostile territories. (Interestingly, neither of these characters has a family himself.) The frustrated narrator of "Bartleby" hits upon the happy expedient of inviting Bartleby to come and live with him for a while, thus exchanging the politicized arena of the office for the (magically) depoliticized arena of home, where conflicts should resolve themselves naturally, in the course of time: " 'Will you go home with me now,' " the narrator asks, " '—not to my office, but my dwelling—and remain there till we can conclude upon some convenient arrangement for you at our leisure?' " Similarly, Captain Delano keeps imaginatively transforming the politically charged world of the slave ship into a cozy domestic scene, in which the blacks play the part of devoted servants, or of devoted Newfoundland dogs.

In Hawthorne and Parkman, we see the family myth used not as a model of accommodation but as a model for an established and secure order that would be violently disrupted by attempts to accommodate those—in this case, the Indians—who do not "naturally" belong to it. If the family myth substitutes similarity for difference, and thus precludes analyses of *kinds* of difference and the hierarchies of power and privilege they produce, then by specifically locating the Indians outside the mythic family, these writers implicitly equate the Indians with difference and, at the same time, with the free play of "unnatural" forms of power. Hawthorne's manipulation of the family myth is clearest in his essay on the Duston family, since there he attempts to direct the reader's interpretation of this episode in the complex history of Indian-white conflicts over territorial rights by using the family as a kind of moveable moral cypher. When the Indians attack the Duston family, they are bloodthirsty savages and the Dustons are innocent victims; when Mrs. Duston takes her revenge on an Indian family, she becomes the savage and the object of

Hawthorne's moral outrage. The political and historical realities that set the Dustons in opposition to the Indians in the first place evaporate in this representation; all that remains are families and the savages who want to destroy them. In *The Scarlet Letter*, the savages appear in the form of the Indians who lurk, threateningly, around the disrupted family that is at the center of the novel. In the metaphoric configuration of the novel, the Indians lurk and threaten precisely because the family has been disrupted and its members have, as a result, become subject to, and victimized by, the forms of power that have free play only outside the stable home.

Parkman's Indians threaten the American family only from a distance, but the threat is nonetheless real. In *The Oregon Trail*, the Indians constitute, collectively, a grotesque and sinister caricature of family: the women are hags, the children are mongrel progeny, and the men are completely lacking in the moral restraint necessary to qualify them for the roles of husband and father. Metaphorically, these Indians inhabit a territory where real, "natural" families do not exist, one that can be safely explored only by the lone male like Parkman. Literally, they inhabit a territory that lies directly in the path of white American expansion, a territory where relationships are deeply politicized and where moral issues become complex and ambiguous in the struggle for dominance. Parkman's representation of the Indians as antithetical to the "natural" family reduces the complex moral issues to a simple formula: mothers, fathers, sons, and daughters do not naturally invite suppression and killing; Indian men and women and their progeny do.

In using Barthes's definition of myth as depoliticized speech, I am, of necessity but also by intention, calling attention to the political content of my own critical statements. By doing so, I put myself in the company of the many other contemporary literary critics who are recognizing that one of the most important and invigorating results of the recent introduction of new theoretical models is that they are providing us with a variety of ways of resituating our critical discourse within a political context. These new models—especially the feminist, Marxist, and new-historicist models—have allowed us to politicize our own speech in fruitful and interesting ways. We have been able, to take one important example, to give issues of race and gender a central place in the (collective) work we do as writers and teachers, rather than leaving them to be "covered" by departments of African-American studies and women's studies. Clearly, however, none of us is ready to declare that trading in our old models for new ones has magically given us perfect insight or guaranteed that all our critical statements will now be unassailable. We know that with new insights come new forms of blindness. We also know that even new models require a lot of road testing and tinkering. There is, in short, little danger that we will stop writing books in which we return to the "classic" texts of American literature and continue to argue with one another about how (or even whether) to read them.

In this book, I have been making the argument, in a fairly generalized way, that one significant blind spot in *most* readings of nineteenth-century American literature has been the failure to take seriously the presence of the American Indians as a factor in the shaping of the literature. I want to end the book by making the assertion that contemporary criticism, even with its emphasis on demythologizing literary discourse and politicizing critical discourse, is still essentially replicating nineteenth-century criticism when it comes to the subject of Indians. Either the Indian presence is ignored, or the Indians are *re*mythologized by the critic. I would even assert that contemporary criticism is still showing signs of the same resistance to speaking about Indians that many nineteenth-century critics expressed—a resistance based (I believe) on the sense that Indians cannot be moved from the margins to the center of sophisticated intellectual discourse; for the critic to attempt to do so is to run the risk of relegating her own discourse to the margins.

To support these assertions, I could offer a list of recent books of cultural, historical, or ideological criticism that include no mention of the Indians in their discussions of nineteenth-century American literature. Instead of attempting to document an absence, however, I want instead to mention briefly four recent books that do include some reference to the Indians, in order to suggest how little the critical response to the presence of Indians in literary texts has changed in 150 years. I choose these four not because I think they are uninteresting books, but, on the contrary, because I think they are, in most respects, interesting, useful, responsible, and important books. I refer to them here because they help to illustrate my point that for many critics, no matter how historically oriented they are or how sensitive they are to issues of race and class, Indianness is *still* taken to be only a naively constructed trope that is usually employed by bad novelists; as soon as Indians appear in a text, that text ceases to be ideologically interesting and complex and starts to become embarrassing.

In her discussion of the kinds of "cultural work" being accomplished in some American novels that she sees as having been inappropriately dismissed as sentimental and therefore not very good, Jane Tompkins addresses the matter of Fenimore Cooper's melodramatic and unconvincing plotting and characterization. To account for his excesses, Tompkins locates Cooper within a novelistic tradition whose stock-in-trade was melodramatic excess. As a way of situating Cooper in American literary history, Tompkins notes (following Louise Barnett) that "between the War of 1812 and the Civil War, Americans wrote seventy-three novels dealing with Indian-white relations. . . . " These seventy-three novels constitute what Tompkins calls the "genre" of "frontier romance"; Cooper's novels now seem predictable, she argues, because he was working within the conventions of this genre—but adapting them to his own complex purposes. Tompkins prefaces these statements about the frontier romance with a discussion of Cooper's preoccupation in his frontier novels with cultural and racial difference, with the gulfs that separate different "kinds" of people. She then raises an interesting question and supplies a surprising answer:

> It is necessary to ask at this point why a meditation on "kinds" should be the subject of an American novel in 1826, and why such a novel should have been written by Cooper. Cooper's preoccupation with questions of national, racial, and ethnic mixing would seem to follow naturally from the multi-ethnic composition of his native New York State.

For Tompkins, then, the way to understand the ubiquitous presence of Indian characters in Cooper's novels is to recognize that he was deliberately *working* a genre that required the inclusion of Indians, that his real concern in 1826 was not the impending crisis of Indian removal but the presence of so many European immigrants in his home state. Cooper's Indian are interesting, therefore, because they really stand in for the Dutch, the Germans, the Irish, and others. And his novels should be taken seriously because, presumably, unlike others of the seventy-three novels that address Indian-white relations, they aren't really about Indians after all.[2]

Eric Sundquist's *Home as Found: Authority and Genealogy in Nineteenth-Century American Literature* offers a brilliant analysis of the American writer's paradoxical desire to rebel against the past (to *found* a new home) and, at the same time, to commemorate the past by replicating it (to *find* the original home). His discussion of Thoreau centers on *A Week on the Concord and Merrimack Rivers* and includes a fairly lengthy analysis of Thoreau's fascination with Indians. However, Sundquist sees this fascination as played out almost entirely in Thoreau's search for Indian relics and for a "pure" Indian language, in both of which Thoreau wished to find traces of the primitive America of his fantasies. Sundquist's conclusion is that "what disturbed Thoreau at first, though in the end probably just bemused him, was that he could not get to the bottom of his search for the Indian, and 'Indian' itself came finally to be almost an empty label for whatever phenomena, artifactual or fantastic, were presently missing from the landscape."[3] My quarrel with Sundquist's discussion of Thoreau and the Indians is that behind his argument are the tacit implications that there *were* no more Indians in the American landscape in 1849, that Thoreau's attitudes toward the Indians were entirely a function of his allegorizing imagination, and that his references to Indians signal only his anxiety about finding a psychological home in his fantasies about the original America and say nothing of his awareness that the new America was, at the moment of his writing, still busily engaged in removing Indians from the landscape. The journey that is recorded in *A Week* took place in 1839, the year after the Trail of Tears (although Thoreau did not publish his book until ten years later). Thoreau knew where the real Indians were and what was happening to them, and he looked for ways to justify what was happening. He also sought out some of the Indians remaining in the East; he just didn't like them much when he found them.

The two other books I want to mention, Lawrence Buell's *New England Literary Culture: From Revolution Through Renaissance* and David Leverenz's *Manhood and the American Renaissance*, approach the "classic" texts of the nineteenth century from very different perspectives. Buell's book is a detailed and magisterially encylopedic survey of intellectual movements in New England and of the institutions that generated and sustained them. Leverenz's study, which focuses on questions of gender construction, is more explicitly theoretical than Buell's. Where the two books are similar is in their almost reflexive distaste for writing in which Indian characters have a prominent role. For both, Indians seem to be simply boring. Buell notes, hurriedly, that "when Indian life is made the central subject of a work, the result is invariably a pasteboard caricature of noble savages or bestial villains. . . ."[4] Leverenz discusses Child's *Hobomok* as a specific example of those books that are too dull to be taken seriously. For him, reading the novel was "an exasperating and dispiriting experience."[5] He mentions Mary Conant's marriage to Hobomok only to declare it a thoroughly uninteresting version of the sentimental heroine's predictable attempt to flee from patriarchal authority; the only function of the marriage, as Leverenz sees it, is that it gives the heroine the chance to flirt with rebellion before returning to a more conventional marriage. In this (dehistoricized) reading, the Indian Hobomok stands only for the generically exotic; he might as well have been a Frenchman or a gypsy.

The point I wish to make here, and it is perhaps the most important point I have to make in this book, is that most of us who teach and write about American literature still do not believe that it is necessary, or even important, to know much about American Indians or about the history and politics of Indian affairs in order to do our teaching and writing confidently and authoritatively. In looking back at the nineteenth century, we recognize that white Americans were experimenting with the invention of one American nation in their literary discourse at the same time they were negotiating the structure of another one in their courts and congresses. We approach the literary discourse—rightly, I believe—as suspicious readers, and we are turning more and more to history, to "materialist" and "new historicist" criticism, to confirm our suspicions about the gap between the two constructions of the nation. But I do not think we have yet turned a fully suspicious eye on our own critical discourse—our own reinventions of the American past. We have experimented with identifying the master narratives of the nineteenth century as attempts to give discursive authority to the myths of patriarchy, of imperialism, of white racism. And yet, we still haven't taken very seriously the presence of the Indians as a crucial factor in the shaping of any of these forms of American mythology. Our sense seems to be that "the Indian question" has been adequately "done," or can be adequately pursued by those who "do" Native American Studies—and a good thing, too. Indians still seem to embarrass most of us, or bore us, or make us feel quite uncritically pious. And these reactions do not translate well into the rhetoric of our critical discourse. It is still difficult, in short, to find a place for the Indians in the "civilized" texts we produce as critics; and the alternative to finding a place there is still, it seems, removal.

Notes

Introduction

1. Calvin Martin, "The Metaphysics of Writing Indian-White History," in *The American Indian and the Problem of History*, ed. Calvin Martin (New York: Oxford University Press, 1987), p. 33.
2. Robert F. Berkhofer, Jr., "Cultural Pluralism versus Ethnocentrism in the New Indian History," in *The American Indian and the Problem of History*, ed. Calvin Martin (New York: Oxford University Press, 1987), pp. 43–44. Compare Michel Foucault's observation that "the cry goes up that one is murdering history whenever, in a historical analysis—and especially if it is concerned with thought, ideas, or knowledge—one is seen to be using in too obvious a way the categories of discontinuity and difference. . . . One will be denounced for attacking the inalienable rights of history and the very foundations of any possible historicity" (*The Archaeology of Knowledge*, trans. A. M. Sheridan Smith [New York: Pantheon Books, 1972], p. 14).
3. Arnold Krupat, "Post-Structuralism and Oral Literature," in *Recovering the Word: Essays on Native American Literature*, ed. Brian Swann and Arnold Krupat (Berkeley: University of California Press, 1987), p. 113. Krupat has been consistently optimistic about the possibilities for combining Indian literatures with Anglo-American literature in a single American canon that would be open to investigation through most forms of structuralist and poststructuralist theory. His book *The*

Voice in the Margin: Native American Literature and the Canon (Berkeley: University of California Press, 1989) is an extended argument for a new "cosmopolitan" and "genuinely heterodox national canon" (p. 232), in which the relationship among canonical texts would be dialogic rather than hierarchical.

4. Elaine Jahner, "A Critical Approach to American Indian Literature," in *Studies in American Indian Literature*, ed. Paula Gunn Allen (New York: Modern Language Association, 1983), p. 212.

5. Gerald Vizenor, "Socioacupuncture: Mythic Reversals and the Striptease," in *The American Indian and the Problem of History*, ed. Calvin Martin (New York: Oxford University Press, 1987), p. 183.

6. Wilcomb E. Washburn, ed., *The American Indian and the United States: A Documentary History* (New York: Random House, 1973), 2:1075.

7. Francis Paul Prucha, *The Great Father: The United States Government and the American Indians* (Lincoln: University of Nebraska Press, 1984), p. 190.

8. Washburn, *The American Indian and the United States*, 1:61.

9. The Smithsonian Institution still (as of this writing) houses its permanent exhibits on the Indians of North America in the Museum of Natural History rather than in the Museum of American History.

10. George Bancroft, *History of the United States*, 2d ed. (Boston: Charles C. Little & James Brown, 1840), 3:265.

11. Washburn, *The American Indian and the United States*, 1:49.

12. The history of Anglo-American privileging of the term *nation* has led some contemporary Indian activists, such as Roxanne Dunbar Ortiz, to declare that "Native American nations prefer not to be referred to as 'tribes' " (*The Great Sioux Nation: Sitting in Judgment on America* [Moon Books/American Treaty Council Information Center, 1977], p. 203).

13. Washburn, *The American Indian and the United States*, 1:62.

Chapter 1

1. Wilcomb E. Washburn, ed., *The American Indian and the United States: A Documentary History* (New York: Random House, 1973), 1:1128.

2. Richard Peters, *The Case of the Cherokee Nation Against the State of Georgia* (Philadelphia: John Grigg, 1831), pp. 150, 160.

3. *American Quarterly Review* 21 (March–June 1832): 1.

4. Frances Trollope, *Domestic Manners of the Americans*, ed. Donald Smalley (New York: Knopf, 1949), p. 221; Ralph Waldo Emerson, "Letter to President Van Buren," *Complete Works*, centenary ed. (Boston: Houghton, Mifflin, 1903–1904), 11:92; Helen Hunt Jackson, *A Century of Dishonor* (New York: Harper, 1965), p. 270.

5. Peter Farb, *Man's Rise to Civilization: The Cultural Ascent of the Indians of North America* (New York: Dutton, 1978), p. 239; James Mooney, *Historical Sketch of the Cherokee* (1900; reprint, Chicago: Aldine, 1975), p. 104.

6. The chief sources I have used for this very brief summary of the complex relations between the Cherokees and the state of Georgia are Mooney, *Historical Sketch of the Cherokee*; Angie Debo, *A History of the Indians of the United States* (Norman: University of Oklahoma Press, 1970); and Ronald N. Satz, "The Cherokee Trail of Tears: A Sesquicentennial Perspective," *Georgia Historical Quarterly* 73 (Fall 1989): 431–66.

7. Peters, *The Case of the Cherokee Nation*, p. 159.

8. Timothy Flint, *Indian Wars of the West* (Cincinnati: E. H. Flint, 1833), pp. 239–40. Washington Irving offered (in 1837) a similar, if somewhat less sunny, vision of a permanent Indian territory existing inviolate between the white settlements of the East and the Far West: "An immense belt of rocky mountains and volcanic plains, several hundred miles in width, must ever remain an irreclaimable wilderness, intervening between the abodes of civilization, and affording a last refuge to the Indian. Here roving tribes of hunters, living in tents or lodges, and following the migrations of the game, may lead a life of savage independence, where there is nothing to tempt the cupidity of the white man" (*The Adventures of Captain Bonneville, U.S.A. in the Rocky Mountains of the Far West* [New York: Spuyten Duyvil, 1849], 2:422).

9. Thomas J. Farnham, *Travels in the Great Western Prairies, the Anahuac and Rocky Mountains, and in the Oregon Territory* (1843; reprint, New York: Da Capo Press, 1973), pp. 115, 116, 117.

10. William Bartram, *Travels of William Bartram*, ed. Mark Van Doren (New York: Dover, 1955), p. 26.

11. Interestingly, many of those who were engaged in missions to the Indians, from the seventeenth century on, argued that the Indians could not be christianized until they had first been civilized. Cotton Mather,

for example, wrote of the most famous Puritan missionary to the Indians, John Eliot, that "he had a double work incumbent on him; he was to make men of them, ere he could hope to see them saints; they must be *civilized* before they could be *Christianized*. . . . " In his book on Indian languages, Roger Williams expressed his hope that more whites would learn to speak to Indians in their own languages, "and by such converse it may please the *Father* of *Mercies* to spread *civilitie*, (and in his owne most holy season *Christianitie*) . . . ." The Moravian missionary John Heckwelder, writing in 1819, echoed Williams when he offered his opinion that "if, instead of employing them to fight our battles, we encouraged them to remain at peace with us and with each other, they might easily be brought to a state of civilization, and become CHRISTIANS." (Cotton Mather, *Magnalia Christi Americana* [New York: Russell & Russell, 1967], 1:560; Roger Williams, *A Key Into the Language of America*, ed. John J. Teunissen and Evelyn J. Hinz [Detroit: Wayne State University Press, 1973], p. 84; John Heckwelder, *An Account of the History, Manners, and Customs of the Indian Nations* [Philadelphia: Abraham Small, 1819], p. 345.)

12. John Kirk Townsend, *Narrative of a Journey Across the Rocky Mountains to the Columbia River*, ed. Donald Jackson (Lincoln: University of Nebraska Press, 1978), pp. 203, 210.

13. Washburn, *The American Indian and the United States*, 1:26, 36, 422.

14. Anthony Pagden, *The Fall of Natural Man: The American Indian and the Origins of Comparative Ethnography* (Cambridge: Cambridge University Press, 1982), p. 18.

15. Jedediah Morse, *A Report to the Secretary of War, of the United States, on Indian Affairs* (1822; reprint, New York: Augustus M. Kelley, 1970), pp. 357, 358–59.

16. Farnham, *Travels in the Great Western Prairies*, p. 172.

17. "The Indians of North America," *North American Review* 22 (1826): 118, 119. The civilization-or-extinction argument was even adopted by the Cherokee spokesman, Elias Boudinot. In a speech given in 1826, Boudinot appealed to the white community for support in establishing a printing press and a seminary for the use of the Cherokees. He concluded his appeal with the reminder that "there are, with regard to the Cherokees and other tribes, two alternatives: they must either become civilized and happy, or sharing the fate of many kindred

nations, become extinct." Elias Boudinott [*sic*], *An Address to the Whites* (Philadelphia: William F. Geddes, 1826), p. 15.

18. *North American Review* 23 (1826): 474.
19. *American Quarterly Review* 8 (1830): 109.
20. *North American Review* 47 (1838): 142.
21. Charles Fenno Hoffman, *A Winter in the West* (New York: Harper & Brothers, 1835), 1:160–62.
22. "Historical Discourse, At Concord, on the Second Centennial Anniversary of the Incorporation of the Town, September 12, 1835," in *The Works of Ralph Waldo Emerson: Miscellanies* (Boston: Fireside, 1909), pp. 64, 54, 55, 56.
23. *North American Review* 53 (1842): 1.
24. Darcy McNickle, *Native American Tribalism* (New York: Oxford University Press, 1973), p. 74; Washburn, *The American Indian and the United States*, 1:36.
25. William L. Stone, *The Life and Times of Red-Jacket* (New York: Wiley & Putnam, 1841), pp. 397, 404.
26. George Catlin, *Letters and Notes on the Manners, Customs, and Conditions of the North American Indians* (New York: Dover, 1973), 1:3, 16, 184.
27. Samuel Parker, *Journal of an Exploring Tour Beyond the Rocky Mountains* (reprint, Minneapolis: Ross & Haines, 1967), pp. 13, 212, 142, 314.
28. *Democratic Review* 11 (1842): 621.
29. *Democratic Review* 14 (1844): 170, 171.
30. Ruth Miller Elson, *Guardians of Tradition: American Schoolbooks of the Nineteenth Century* (Lincoln: University of Nebraska Press, 1964), pp. 69, 79.
31. See Frank Edgar Farley, "The Dying Indian," in *Anniversary Papers by Colleagues and Pupils of George Lyman Kittredge* (New York: Russell & Russell, 1913), pp. 251–60.
32. *Southern Literary Messenger* 11 (1845): 537–39.
33. See Reginald Horsman, "Scientific Racism and the American Indian in the Mid-Nineteenth Century," *American Quarterly Review* 27 (May 1975): 152–68.
34. My citations are taken from p. 338 of the review, which appears in the *Democratic Review* 26 n.s. (1850): 327–45.
35. William Gilmore Simms, *Charlemont: or, The Pride of the Village* (reprint, New York: AMS Press, 1970), p. 14.

36. James Hall, *The Wilderness and the Warpath* (reprint, New York: Garrett Press, 1969), p. 34.

37. "The Social Condition of Women," reprinted in *Essays from the North American Review*, ed. Allen Thorndike Rice (New York: Appleton, 1879), p. 69.

38. Lady [Sydney] Morgan, *Woman and Her Master* (Philadelphia: Carey & Hart, 1840), 1:25–26.

39. Margaret Fuller, *Summer on the Lakes, in 1843* (Boston: Charles C. Little & James Brown, 1844), p. 179; Mary Eastman, *Dahcotah: Or, Life and Legends of the Sioux* (New York: Wiley, 1849), pp.iv–v.

40. Washburn, *The American Indian and the United States*, 1:54, 61.

41. Ibid., 2:54.

42. Cited in Dee Brown, *Bury My Heart at Wounded Knee* (New York: Bantam, 1972), p. 153.

43. Cathy N. Davidson, *Revolution and the Word: The Rise of the Novel in America* (New York: Oxford University Press, 1986), p. 41.

44. William Gilmore Simms, *Views and Reviews in American Literature, History and Fiction, First Series*, ed. C. Hugh Holman (Cambridge: Harvard University Press, 1962), pp. 21, 10, 112.

45. Ibid., pp. 84, 138.

46. Robert Strange, *Eoneguski, or The Cherokee Chief* (Washington: Franck Taylor, 1839; reprint, Charlotte, NC: McNally, 1960), p. xi.

47. *American Quarterly Review* 8 (1830): 123.

48. *New-England Magazine* 6 (1834): 512; 8 (1835): 236.

49. Simms, *Views and Reviews*, pp. 84, 16, 34.

50. Ibid., p. 139.

51. Morse, *A Report to the Secretary of War*, pp. 74–75. Morse's advice was specific:

> While Indians remain in their present state, the minds of civilized people must revolt at the idea of intermarrying with them. . . . It is essential to the success of the project of the Government, that the female character among our native tribes, be raised from its present degraded state, to its proper rank and influence. This should be a *primary* object with the instructors of Indians. . . . Thus educated, and the marriage institution, in its purity, introduced, the principal obstacles to intermarriage with them would be removed. . . .

52. *North American Review* 23 (1826): 474.

53. *North American Review* 18 (1824): 263.

54. Simms, *Views and Reviews*, p. 112. Simms goes on to offer a specific

example of an inviting subject for the American artist (in this case, the painter) in the story of John Smith and the virgin Pocahontas. In Simms's envisioning of the scene, Smith, with his "manly cheek," "eagle eye," and "muscular form," is saved from death by "that loveliest creation of mortal beauty, a young girl just budding into womanhood" (pp. 118, 119).

55. Cited in Richard Ruland, *The Native Muse: Theories of American Literature* (New York: Dutton, 1972), p. 291.

56. Cornelius Mathews, *Behemoth: A Legend of the Mound-Builders* (1846; reprint, New York: AMS Press, 1971), p. 91.

57. Washington Irving, *The Sketchbook of Geoffrey Crayon, Esq.*, ed. Haskell Springer (Boston: Twayne, 1978), p. 225.

58. Caroline Kirkland, preface to *Dahcotah: Or, Life and Legends of the Sioux*, by Mary Eastman (New York: Wiley, 1849) pp. vi, viii, x.

59. *North American Review* 26 (1828): 418.

60. *New-England Magazine* 6 (January–June, 1834): 525.

61. *Southern Literary Messenger* 11 (1845): 734.

62. *North American Review* 47 (1838): 137, 138. Bayard Taylor echoed this position in an 1858 letter written to Longfellow. Taylor expressed his conviction that Indian legends, such as those Longfellow adapted in *Hiawatha*, are usually "repulsive to the sympathies of our race and the taste of our times." He went on to commend Longfellow for "representing the purely poetical aspects of Indian life and tradition, concealing what is gross and repulsive, yet without destroying the fidelity of the picture" (*Life of Henry Wadsworth Longfellow*, ed. Samuel Longfellow [Boston: Ticknor, 1886], 2:264).

63. *Democratic Review* 11 (1842): 644.

64. Ralph Waldo Emerson, *Essays and Lectures* (New York: Library of America, 1983), p. 1222.

65. In an 1855 letter to Longfellow, Emerson responded to the publication of *Hiawatha* with much stronger and more specific language than he had used in the 1842 review of Colton's poem. Emerson congratulated Longfellow on his success in making the poem "sweet and wholesome as maize" and in making his Indian characters presentable to the reading public. "The dangers of the Indian are," Emerson wrote, "that they are really savage, have poor, small, sterile heads,—no thoughts; and you must deal very roundly with them, and find them in brains" (Longfellow, *Life of Henry Wadsworth Longfellow*, 2:266).

66. *North American Review* 63 (1846): 360.
67. *North American Review* 46 (1828): 376.
68. *New-England Magazine* 8 (1835): 489–90.
69. For an excellent discussion of Cooper and romance, see Robert Clark, *History, Ideology and Myth in American Fiction, 1823–52* (London: Methuen, 1984).
70. Francis Parkman, "James Fenimore Cooper," reprinted in Rice, *Essays from the North American Review*, pp. 363, 374.
71. *North American Review* 64 (1849): 208.

Chapter 2

1. Jay Leyda, *The Melville Log: A Documentary Life of Herman Melville, 1819–1891* (New York: Harcourt, Brace, 1951), 1:474.
2. *The Literature of the American People*, ed. Arthur Hobson Quinn (New York: Appleton-Century-Crofts, 1951), p. 243.
3. Michael Paul Rogin, *Subversive Genealogy: The Politics and Art of Herman Melville* (New York: Knopf, 1983), p. 41.
4. George Catlin, *Letters and Notes on the Manners, Customs, and Conditions of the North American Indians* (New York: Dover, 1973), 1:184.
5. Wilcomb E. Washburn, ed., *The American Indian and the United States: A Documentary History* (New York: Random House, 1973), 2:1235–36.
6. Herman Melville, "Hawthorne and His Mosses," in *The Piazza Tales and Other Prose Pieces, 1839–1860*, ed. Harrison Hayford et al. (Evanston and Chicago: Northwestern University Press and the Newberry Library, 1987), p. 246.
7. Tzvetan Todorov, *The Conquest of America: The Question of the Other*, trans. Richard Howard (New York: Harper & Row, 1985), pp. 42–43.
8. Melville, "Hawthorne and His Mosses," p. 244.
9. *Democratic Review* 12 (1843): 403.
10. Herman Melville, *Typee: A Peep at Polynesian Life*, ed. Harrison Hayford et al. (Evanston and Chicago: Northwestern University Press and the Newberry Library, 1968), pp. 26–27. References to this edition are given parenthetically in the text.
11. Herman Melville, *Moby-Dick, or the Whale*, ed. Charles Feidelson, Jr. (New York: Bobbs-Merrill, 1964), p. 181. References to this edition are given parenthetically in the text.

12. Herman Melville, *The Confidence-Man: His Masquerade*, ed. Hershel Parker (New York: Norton, 1971), p. 131. References to this edition are given parenthetically in the text.

13. Herman Melville, *Pierre, or the Ambiguities*, ed. Harrison Hayford et al. (Evanston and Chicago: Northwestern University Press and the Newberry Library, 1971), p. 138. References to this edition are given parenthetically in the text.

14. References to "Bartleby" and "Benito Cereno," which are given parenthetically in the text, are from Herman Melville, *The Piazza Tales and Other Prose Pieces, 1839–1860*, ed. Harrison Hayford et al. (Evanston and Chicago: Northwestern University Press and the Newberry Library, 1971).

15. William L. Stone, *Life of Joseph Brant—Thayendanegea* (New York: Alexander V. Blake, 1838), 1:xiii. Stone's book was one that Melville knew well, since it records the military exploits of Peter Gansevoort, Melville's maternal grandfather, who fought against Brant at the siege of Fort Stanwix. Melville referred his friend Evert Duycinck to the book in a letter explaining to Duyckinck why he had named his new-born son Stanwix (Leyda, *The Melville Log*, 1:432).

16. Washington Irving, *The Sketchbook of Geoffrey Crayon, Esq.* ed. Haskell Springer (Boston: Twayne, 1978), p. 233.

17. Herman Melville, "The Apple-Tree Table," in *The Piazza Tales and Other Prose Pieces, 1839–1860*, ed. Harrison Hayford et al. (Evanston and Chicago: Northwestern University Press and the Newberry Library, 1971), p. 383.

18. Richard Slotkin, *Regeneration Through Violence: The Mythology of the American Frontier, 1600–1860* (Middletown, Conn.: Wesleyan University Press, 1973), p. 136.

19. Cotton Mather, *Magnalia Christi Americana* (New York: Russell & Russell, 1967), 2:552, 555.

20. Edward Johnson, *Johnson's Wonder-Working Providence*, ed. J. Franklin Jameson (New York: Scribner's, 1910), p. 164.

21. Increase Mather and Cotton Mather, *The History of King Philip's War*, ed. Samuel G. Drake (Albany: J. Munsell, 1862), pp. 196, 197.

22. Samuel G. Drake, *Biography and History of the Indians of North America*, 4th ed. (Boston: J. Drake, 1835), bk. 3, p. 61; bk. 2, pp. 81–82. Drake's book was first published in 1832 and was then revised and enlarged in several successive editions.

23. Benjamin Church, *Diary of King Philip's War 1675–76*, ed. Alan and Mary Simpson (Chester, Conn.: Pequot Press, 1975), p. 139.

24. Edwin Fussell has written that "Melville's most inclusive intention is constantly to insinuate some sort of sly connection between Ahab's business with the White Whale and America's business with the Far West" (*Frontier: American Literature and the American West* [Princeton: Princeton University Press, 1965], p. 261).

25. Herman Melville, "Mr. Parkman's Tour," in *The Piazza Tales and Other Prose Pieces 1839–1860*, ed. Haskell Springer (Evanston and Chicago: Northwestern University Press and the Newberry Library, 1971), p. 232. The review was originally published in the *Literary World* 4 (March 31, 1849): 291–93.

26. *Harper's New Monthly Magazine* 2 (December 1850–May 1851): 701.

27. Gary Lindberg, *The Confidence Man in Literature* (New York: Oxford University Press, 1982), p. 150.

28. Thomas L. McKenney, *Memoirs, Official and Personal* (New York: Paine & Burgess, 1846), 1:20. References to this edition are given parenthetically in the text.

29. Michael Paul Rogin has also noted (in *Subversive Genealogy*) that the McKenney-McDonald relationship resembles the narrator-Bartleby relationship.

30. Melville, "Mr. Parkman's Tour," p. 231.

31. Melville's narrator and McKenney even use the same specific metaphor to represent the ultimate failure of their undertakings. The narrator ends his account with a reflection on the years Bartleby spent as a clerk in the Dead Letter Office, and McKenney complains that the Indian Civilization Act of 1819, which was essentially his project, "was destined, at last, though unrepealed, to become a dead letter!" (*Memoirs, Official and Personal* [1:258]).

32. *The Works of Washington Irving* (New York: G. P. Putnam's Sons, 1849), 2:161. References to this edition of *Astoria* are given parenthetically in the text.

33. Leyda, *The Melville Log*, 1:475.

34. Merton M. Sealts notes that "the supporting characters [in "Bartleby"] could easily have come from the pen of Dickens, Lamb, or Irving." Sealts names Irving as one influence on Melville's short fiction but does not indicate that he sees Melville as in any way a *resisting* reader of Irving. He concludes only that when Melville turned from novel-

writing to story-writing, he "found Irving a useful model" (*Melville's Reading* [University of South Carolina Press, 1988], pp. 89, 90).

35. J. Luther Ringwalt, *American Encyclopedia of Printing* (Philadelphia: Lippincott, 1871).

36. Eric J. Sundquist, "Benito Cereno and New World Slavery," in *Reconstructing American Literary History*, ed. Sacvan Bercovitch (Cambridge: Harvard University Press, 1986), p. 102.

37. Ralph Waldo Emerson, "Nature," in *The Complete Essays and Other Writings of Ralph Waldo Emerson*, ed. Brooks Atkinson (New York: Modern Library, 1950), pp. 6, 3.

38. See Church, *Diary of King Philip's War*, pp. 134–36.

39. Catlin, *Letters and Notes on the Manners, Customs and Conditions of the North American Indians*, 2:159.

40. Ibid., p. 219n.

41. See *The Confidence-Man*, ed. Harrison Hayford et al. (Evanston and Chicago: Northwestern University Press and The Newberry Library, 1984), pp. 340–42, for a summary of the basic issues that have divided critics of the Indian-hating section. Most of the critics have agreed that the section is meant to be read as allegory; the disagreements have come on the question of which figure Melville saw as Satanic—the Indian or the Indian-hater. For a very good rebuttal to the argument that the section is an allegory of good and evil, see Joyce Adler, "Melville on the White Man's War Against the American Indians," *Science and Society* 36 (Winter 1972): 417–42.

42. Cadwallader Colden, *The History of the Five Indian Nations* (Ithaca: Cornell University Press, 1980), p. 12.

43. *Democratic Review* 12 (1843): 403.

44. Francis Parkman, *The Conspiracy of Pontiac* (New York: Dutton, n.d.), 1:30.

45. Carolyn L. Karcher, *Shadow over the Promised Land: Slavery, Race, and Violence in Melville's America* (Baton Rouge: Louisiana State University Press, 1980), p. 257.

Chapter 3

1. *The Works of Rufus Choate*, ed. Samuel Gilman Brown (Boston: Little, Brown, 1862), 1:319, 333.

2. Among the most popular treatments of King Philip's War produced before 1833 were a long poem by James W. Eastburn and Robert C.

Sands, *Yamoyden, A Tale of the Wars of King Philip,* published in 1820, and John Augustus Stone's 1829 play, *Metamora, or the Last of the Wampanoags.* James Fenimore Cooper had also treated the aftermath of the war in *The Wept of Wish-ton-Wish* (1829).

3. Choate's equating of sunlight with the perspective of romance and starlight with the perspective of historical writing may seem especially naive to us because we have so fully accepted Hawthorne's definition of romance (in "The Custom House") as a moonlight medium. In one of his early sketches of Puritan history, however, Hawthorne proposed a definition of romance that is very close to Choate's:

> The knowledge communicated by the historians and biographers is analogous to that which we acquire of a country by the map,—minute, perhaps, and accurate, and available for all necessary purposes, but cold and naked, and wholly destitute of the mimic charm produced by landscape painting. . . . A license must be assumed in brightening the materials which time has rusted, and in tracing out half-obliterated inscriptions on the columns of antiquity: Fancy must throw her reviving light on the faded incidents that indicate character, whence a ray will be reflected, more or less vividly, on the person to be described. ("Sir William Phips," in *The Complete Writings of Nathaniel Hawthorne* [Boston: Houghton Mifflin, 1900], 17:13)

4. Lawrence Buell, *New England Literary Culture: From Revolution to Renaissance* (New York: Cambridge University Press, 1986), p. 211.

5. Catherine Maria Sedgwick, *Hope Leslie: or, Early Times in the Massachusetts,* ed. Mary Kelley (New Brunswick: Rutgers University Press, 1987), p. 5. Further references to this edition are given parenthetically in the text.

6. Lydia Maria Child, *Hobomok and Other Writings on Indians,* ed. Carolyn L. Karcher (New Brunswick: Rutgers University Press 1986), pp. 3–4. Further references to this edition are given parenthetically in the text.

7. Nathaniel Hawthorne, *The Scarlet Letter* (New York: Penguin Books, 1983), p. 63. Further references to this edition are given parenthetically in the text.

8. William R. Hutchinson, *The Transcendentalist Ministers: Church Reform in the New England Renaissance* (New Haven: Yale University Press 1959), p. 5.

9. Anita Levy, "Blood, Kinship, and Gender," *Genders,* no. 5 (Summer 1989), p. 70.

10. Child took the name of her friendly Indian from the historical Hobomok

(or Hobbamock), and her fictitious character shows some resemblance to the original Wampanoag chief. The actual Hobomok settled in Plymouth, befriending the English there and acting as a mediator between them and the sachem Massasoit. Unlike Child's character, however, he converted to Christianity and spent the end of his life living peacefully among the white population of Plymouth. Child probably used his name to take advantage of his reputation as a reliable "friend-Indian."

11. Carolyn L. Karcher, introduction to *Hobomok and Other Writings on Indians*, by Lydia Maria Child, ed. Carolyn L. Karcher (New Brunswick: Rutgers University Press, 1986), p. xxxii.

12. *Lydia Maria Child: Selected Letters, 1817–1880*, ed. Milton Meltzer and Patricia G. Holland (Amherst: University of Massachusetts Press, 1982), p. 327.

13. Lydia Maria Child, "An Appeal for the Indians," in her *Hobomok and Other Writings on Indians*, ed. Carolyn L. Karcher (New Brunswick: Rutgers University Press, 1986), pp. 221, 220.

14. Sedgwick, like Child, bases some of her Indian characters very loosely on their historical originals. Magawisca is evidently Sedgwick's own invention, but the story of her father, Mononotto, does have some basis in fact. Mononotto was a Pequod chief whose village was attacked by the English early in the Pequod War. His wife and children were taken captive, but because the wife had previously been instrumental in saving the lives of two young English girls, she and her children were turned over to John Winthrop and probably became servants. Sedgwick uses these details in the novel, but adds the subsequent life histories of Mononotto's captive children and even of Mononotto himself, whom the historians believe to have been killed by the English shortly after the end of the Pequod War.

15. *North American Review* 19 (1824): 263.

16. My reading of Magawisca differs from that of Michael Davitt Bell, who sees her as a conventional dark heroine, the rival of the fair Hope Leslie. For Bell, Magawisca "represents the perils of nature"; her own nature is "wild and dangerous; it must be rejected before the final marriage of hero and heroine" ("History and Romance Convention in Catherine Sedgwick's *Hope Leslie*," *American Quarterly* 22 [Summer 1970]: 218–19).

17. In singling out vengefulness as the attribute that most distinguishes

the unreconstructed Indian "nature," Sedgwick agrees with the conclusions of the Moravian missionary John Heckwelder. Even though he defended the Indians against charges that they were savages who could not be civilized and urged sending more missionaries among them, Heckwelder still admitted that the "passion of revenge" in the Indians posed a difficult problem: "They are, it is true, revengeful to their enemies, to those who wilfully do them an injury, who insult, abuse, or treat them with contempt. It may be said, indeed, that the passion of revenge is so strong in them that it knows no bounds. This does not, however, proceed from a bad or malicious disposition, but from the violence of natural feelings unchecked by social institutions, and unsubdued by the force of revealed religion" (*An Account of the History, Manners, and Customs of the Indian Nations*, [Philadelphia: Abraham Small, 1819] p. 277). Heckwelder's sympathetic account of the Indians was controversial enough to make his book widely known, and it is therefore likely that Sedgwick had read it or at least read reviews and summaries of it.

18. *John Eliot's Indian Dialogues*, ed. Henry W. Bowden and James P. Ronda (Westport, Conn.: Greenwood Press, 1980), pp. 63, 70; Richard W. Cogley, "John Eliot and the Origins of the American Indians," *Early American Literature* 21 (Winter 1986): 214; Samuel G. Drake, *Biography and History of the Indians of North America*, 4th ed. (Boston: J. Drake, 1835) bk. 2, p. 111.

19. Cotton Mather, *Magnalia Christi Americana* (New York: Russell & Russell, 1967), 1:560.

20. Nathaniel Hawthorne, *The Letters, 1813–1843*, ed. Thomas Woodson et al., centenary ed. (Columbus: Ohio State University Press, 1984), p. 558.

21. *The Life of Franklin Pierce*, in *The Complete Writings of Nathaniel Hawthorne*, 17:165–66.

22. Hawthorne's views on moral reform echo those put forward in a critique of Unitarianism that appeared in the *Dial* in 1841. Having attacked the Unitarians for their intellectuality and lack of focus, the writer of the essay concludes with a curt dismissal of their faith in reform: "Nothing real is ever thus effected by main force. Changes in the church and society come not of the flesh, neither by the will of man, but by the will of God" ("The Unitarian Movement in New England," *Dial* 1 [April 1841]: 443).

23. Nathaniel Hawthorne, *The American Notebooks*, ed. Claude M. Simpson (Centenary Edition, 1972), p. 169.

24. Nathaniel Hawthorne, *The Whole History of Grandfather's Chair* (Boston: Houghton Mifflin, 1900), pp. 49–50, 55–57.

25. In his essay "An Ontario Steamboat," Hawthorne expresses his dismay at the condition of a boatload of immigrants who arrive in North America "far ruder and wilder beings than they had embarked; and afterwards, thrown homeless upon the wharves of Quebec and Montreal, and left to wander whither they might, and subsist how they could, it was impossible for their moral natures not to have become woefully deranged and debased" (*The Complete Writings of Nathaniel Hawthorne* [Boston: Houghton Mifflin, 1900], 17:215.)

26. "Mrs. Hutchinson," in *The Complete Writings of Nathaniel Hawthorne*, (Boston: Houghton Mifflin, 1900), 17:1–2.

27. Ibid., p. 7.

28. "The Duston Family," in *The Complete Writings of Nathaniel Hawthorne*, (Boston: Houghton Mifflin, 1900), 17:229–38.

29. In his discussion of the essay on Hannah Duston, Leslie Fiedler concludes that for Hawthorne, Mrs. Duston is "just another avatar of the termagant wife, who in a later incarnation becomes Dame Van Winkle." Fiedler sees Hawthorne as using the essay primarily to praise Mr. Duston, the long-suffering and valiant husband of a shrewish wife. (*The Return of the Vanishing American* [New York: Stein & Day, 1968], p. 103.)

30. Nathaniel Hawthorne, *Twice-Told Tales*, centenary Ed., (Columbus: Ohio State University Press, 1974), pp. 85, 95.

31. Michael J. Colacurcio has made a similar argument, in pointing out that in his portraits of Ann Hutchinson and Hester Prynne, Hawthorne presents female sexuality as "both a source for and a type of individualistic nullification of social restraint." ("Footsteps of Ann Hutchinson: The Context of *The Scarlet Letter*," *ELH* 39 (September 1972): 472.

32. Sacvan Bercovitch has also noted the similarity between Hester's advice to women and Hawthorne's advice to abolitionists in the Pierce biography. See his "A-Politics in *The Scarlet Letter*," *New Literary History* Spring 1988, p. 648.

33. In his phrasing of Hester's new credo, Hawthorne may have been responding directly to George Ripley, the founder of Brook Farm, who

intended his experiment in reform to "prepare a society of liberal, intelligent and cultivated persons, whose relations with each other would permit a more wholesome and simple life than can be led amidst the pressures of our competitive institutions." Cited in James R. Mellow, *Nathaniel Hawthorne in His Times* (Boston: Houghton Mifflin, 1980), p. 178.

34. Mary Rowlandson, "The Soveraignty and Goodness of God, Together with the Faithfulness of His Promises Displayed; Being a Narrative of the Captivity and Restauration of Mrs. Mary Rowlandson," in *Held Captive by Indians: Selected Narratives, 1642–1836*, ed. Richard VanDerBeets (Knoxville: University of Tennessee Press, 1973), p. 64.

35. *The Works of Nathaniel Hawthorne* (Boston: Houghton Mifflin, 1883), 5:457.

36. Hawthorne, *The Letters, 1813–1843*, p. 624.

37. Byron L. Stay has argued that the Eliot's pulpit setting in *Blithedale* is an unironic allusion to all the positive aspects of Puritanism represented by Eliot: "Hawthorne uses the wilderness setting of Eliot's Pulpit to represent Puritan strength in order to contrast the Blithedalers with their seventeenth-century counterparts. . . . The characters of *The Blithedale Romance* fail utterly to live up to the model established by John Eliot." My argument is that in failing utterly as reformers, the Blithedalers *do* live up to the model of Eliot. ("Hawthorne's Fallen Puritans: Eliot's Pulpit in *The Blithedale Romance*," *Studies in the Novel* 18 [Fall 1986]: 284, 289.)

38. *The Works of Nathaniel Hawthorne*, 11:317. Further references to this edition are given parenthetically in the text.

39. Nathaniel Hawthorne, *Mosses from an Old Manse*, (centenary Ed. (Columbus: Ohio State University Press, 1974), p. 11.

Chapter 4

1. "Emerson's Essays," in *The Writings of Margaret Fuller*, ed. Mason Wade (New York: Viking Press, 1941), p. 390.

2. Margaret Fuller, *Summer on the Lakes, in 1843* (Boston: Charles C. Little & James Brown, 1844), p. 189. Further references to this edition are given parenthetically in the text.

3. Henry David Thoreau, *The Maine Woods* (Boston: Houghton Mifflin, 1906), p. 4. Further references to this edition are given parenthetically in the text.

4. *The Correspondence of Henry David Thoreau*, ed. Walter Harding and Carl Bode (New York: New York University Press, 1958), p. 504.

5. Robert F. Sayre, *Thoreau and the American Indians* (Princeton: Princeton University Press, 1977), pp. 121, 122, 119.

6. *Letters of Francis Parkman*, ed. Wilbur R. Jacobs (Norman: University of Oklahoma Press, 1960), 1:23, 35.

7. Francis Parkman, Jr., *The Oregon Trail*, ed. David Levin (New York: Penguin, n.d.), p. 34. Further references to this edition are given parenthetically in the text.

8. Tzvetan Todorov, *The Conquest of America: The Question of the Other*, trans. Richard Howard (New York: Harper & Row, 1985), p. 13.

9. Jacobs, *Letters of Francis Parkman*, 1:23.

10. As Reginald Horsman notes, "By the 1830s pro-Indian and antislavery spokesmen were drawn almost exclusively from areas in which there were few blacks and fewer Indians. It was much easier to take a high moral tone in Boston than in Nashville or Mobile" (*Race and Manifest Destiny: The Origins of American Racial Anglo-Saxonism* [Cambridge: Harvard University Press, 1981], p. 300).

11. In the notes to his edition of *The Oregon Trail* (Madison: University of Wisconsin Press, 1969), E. N. Feltskog suggests that "Outalissi" is probably "Outacity, or Outaissi, the famous Cherokee chief who visited England in 1762 whose portrait was painted by Sir Joshua Reynolds. On the night before he sailed for England, he made a farewell speech to his tribesmen with a moving eloquence that was remembered half a century later by Thomas Jefferson" (416).

12. Margaret Fuller, *Woman in the Nineteenth Century* (New York: Norton, 1971), p. 25. Further references to this edition are given parenthetically in the text.

13. In a review she wrote for the *New York Tribune* of June 28, 1845, Fuller expressed a somewhat more hopeful view of the future of American Indians: "It is easy enough to see why our red man, to whom the white extends the Bible or crucifix with one hand, and the rum-bottle with the other, should look upon Jesus as only one more Manitou, and learn nothing from his precepts or the civilization connected with them. . . . Better days are coming, we do hope, as to these matters— days in which the new shall be harmonized with the old, rather than violently rent asunder from it; when progress shall be accomplished by gentle evolution, as the stem of the plant grows up, rather than by the blasting of rocks, and blindness or death of the miners" (cited

in Bell Gale Chevigny, *The Woman and the Myth: Margaret Fuller's Life and Writings* [Old Westbury, N.Y.: Feminist Press, 1976], pp. 343–44).

14. "American Literature," in Wade, *The Writings of Margaret Fuller*, (New York: Viking Press, 1941), p. 358.

15. Ibid., p. 383.

16. "Modern British Poets," in Wade, *The Writings of Margaret Fuller* (New York: Viking Press, 1941), p. 339.

17. Fuller's allusion is to a famous anecdote about the painter Benjamin West, who is said to have exclaimed, on seeing the Apollo Belvedere in the Vatican, "By God, a Mohawk!"

18. Henry David Thoreau, *A Week on the Concord and Merrimack Rivers* (Boston: Houghton Mifflin, 1893), p. 401. Further references to this edition are given parenthetically in the text.

19. Henry David Thoreau, *Walden* (Boston: Houghton Mifflin, 1906), p. 100. Further references to this edition are given parenthetically in the text.

20. Thoreau goes on in this passage to say that "however much we may admire the orator's occasional bursts of eloquence, the noblest written words are commonly as far behind or above the fleeting spoken language as the firmament with its stars is behind the clouds" (113). The reference to oratory suggests that in the passage as a whole Thoreau is arguing with Cicero's defense of the orator's eloquence, that is, of the power of spoken language, as the source of human superiority over the brute creation. "What other power," Cicero asks, "could have been strong enough . . . to lead [humanity] out of its brutish existence in the wilderness up to our present condition of civilization as men and as citizens . . . ?" (*De Oratore*, I.viii.33).

21. Robert F. Sayre demonstrates convincingly, in *Thoreau and the American Indians*, that *A Week* is organized as a condensed history of Indian-white relations in America and that the image of "the Indian" in that book is of a thoroughly romanticized, ideal manifestation of the primitive. I have not tried to recapitulate Sayre's argument, which I find persuasive and very useful, because I want to focus on those aspects of Thoreau's treatment of the Indians that Sayre does not discuss.

22. *The Writings of Henry David Thoreau: Journal*, ed. Bradford Torrey (Boston: Houghton Mifflin, 1906), 1:253, 445. Further references to this edition are given parenthetically in the text.

23. The letter is cited in "Introductory Note," Thoreau, *The Maine Woods*, pp. x–xi.

24. Eric Sundquist has made a similar point about the paradoxical nature of Thoreau's quest for a "pure" Indian speech. As Sundquist points out, Thoreau's writing affirms that "the only Indian language that is pure is the one that is unintelligible. . . . " (*Home as Found: Authority and Genealogy in Nineteenth-Century American Literature* [Baltimore: Johns Hopkins University Press, 1979], p. 54).

25. Francis Parkman, *The Conspiracy of Pontiac and the Indian War after the Conquest of Canada* (New York: Dutton, n.d.), 1:29–30. Further references to this edition are given parenthetically in the text.

26. Francis Parkman, "James Fenimore Cooper," in *Essays from the North American Review*, ed. Allen Thorndike Rice (New York: Appleton, 1879), p. 361. Parkman admired Cooper's style and his portraits of white men; his Indian characters, on the other hand, Parkman found "for the most part either superficially or falsely drawn" (363).

27. "Adventures on the Prairies," *North American Review* 69 (1849): 177.

28. David Levin, *History as Romantic Art* (Stanford: Stanford University Press, 1959), p. 9. Levin goes on to say this about Parkman and his contemporaries: "Committed to the idea of re-creating the Past, and considering himself a man of letters, the romantic historian did not think about a historical controversy or historical period and then say, 'I shall investigate this subject and find out what happened.' He was more likely to say, 'No history (or no good history) exists in English on this subject. The theme is grand, interesting, novel.' . . . Whatever value facts had for their own sake, it was the story, and the kind of story, that counted" (22).

29. In August of 1845, an editorial writer for the *New York Tribune* noted that ten thousand people had left for Oregon that year, and then expressed his opinion of the movement succinctly: "Was there ever such fatuity short of suicide?" Reprinted in *Niles National Register* 68 (March–September 1845): 339.

30. David Leverenz has also discussed Parkman's pleasure in killing buffalo and his contempt for Indians in *Manhood and the American Renaissance* (Ithaca: Cornell University Press, 1989), pp. 217–26. Leverenz's reading differs significantly from mine, however, since he sees in Parkman's aggression only a sign of his grim obsession with defining his own manhood, his need to assert a ruthless will to dominance. Although I don't disagree with that reading, I find that its

concentration on gender and its almost complete disregard for the issue of race makes the interpretation incomplete. *The Oregon Trail* is intriguingly masculinist, but it is simultaneously disturbingly racist. It seems to me crucially important that when one discusses the exercise of a will to dominance, one must also consider who receives the dominance.

Conclusion

1. Roland Barthes, *Mythologies*, trans. Annette Lavers (New York: Hill & Wang, 1972), pp. 143, 129, 101.

2. Louise Barnett, *The Ignoble Savage: American Literary Racism, 1790– 1890* (Westport, Conn: Greenwood Press, 1975); Jane Tompkins, *Sensational Designs: The Cultural Work of American Fiction, 1790– 1860* (New York: Oxford University Press, 1985), p. 106.

3. Eric Sundquist, *Home as Found: Authority and Genealogy in Nine- teenth-Century American Literature* (Baltimore: Johns Hopkins University Press, 1979), p. 48.

4. Lawrence Buell, *New England Literary Culture: From Revolution Through Renaissance* (New York: Cambridge University Press, 1986), p. 212.

5. David Leverenz, *Manhood and the American Renaissance* (Ithaca: Cornell University Press, 1989), p. 175.

Index